Contents

Helion & Company Limited
Unit 8 Amherst Business Centre
Budbrooke Road
Warwick
CV34 5WE
England
Tel. 01926 499 619
Email: info@helion.co.uk
Website: www.helion.co.uk
Twitter: @helionbooks
Visit our blog http://blog.helion.co.uk/

Designed and typeset by Farr out Publications, Wokingham, Berkshire
Cover design by Paul Hewitt, Battlefield Design (www.battlefield-design.co.uk)

ISBN 978-1-914377-00-6

British Library Cataloguing-in-Publication Data
A catalogue record for this book is available from the British Library

We always welcome receiving book proposals from prospective authors.

Note: In order to simplify the use of this book, all names, locations and geographic designations are as provided in *The Times World Atlas*, or other traditionally accepted major sources of reference, as of the time of described events. Correspondingly, the term 'Congo' designates the area of the former Belgian colony of the Congo Free State, granted independence as the Democratic Republic of the Congo in June 1960 and in use until 1971 when the country was renamed Republic of Zaire, which, in turn, reverted to Democratic Republic of the Congo in 1997, and which remains in use today. As such, Congo is not to be mistaken for the former French colony of Middle Congo (Moyen Congo), officially named the Republic of the Congo on its independence in August 1960, also known as Congo-Brazzaville.

Abbreviations

CEME *Chefe do Estado-Maior do Exército* (Chief of Staff of the Army)
CEMGFA *Chefe do Estado-Maior General das Forças Armadas* (Chief of Staff of the Armed Forces)
CSDN *Conselho Superior de Defesa Nacional* (Supreme Council for National Defence)
FAP *Força Aérea Portuguesa* (Portuguese Air Force)
FLNG *Front de Liberation National de la Guinée* (National Front for the Liberation of Guinea)
FLING *Frente de Libertação e Independência Nacional da Guiné* (National Liberation and Independence Front of Guinea)
LDG *Lancha de Desembarque Grande* (Large Landing Craft)
LFG *Lancha de Fiscalização Grande* (Large Surveillance Boat)
PAIGC *Partido Africano da Independência da Guiné e Cabo Verde* (African Party for the Independence of Guinea and Cape Verde)
PIDE *Polícia Internacional e de Defesa do Estado* (International and State Defence Police)
RTP *Radio Televisão Portuguesa* (Radio Television Portugal)

Introduction

In the early hours of 22 November 1970, six Portuguese warships surrounded Conakry, the capital of the Republic of Guinea on the West African coast. Taking advantage of the darkness of the night, a military force landed on the northern and southern coasts of the sleeping city. At the head of these men was a young Portuguese marine officer, Commander Alpoim Calvão, who had been appointed to command this secret operation, codenamed Green Sea – *Mar Verde* in Portuguese. The main objective of the invasion was to promote a coup d'état in the former French colony and overthrow the government of President Sékou Touré, who supported the guerrillas of the PAIGC (African Party for the Independence of Guinea and Cape Verde), who were fighting for the independence of Portuguese Guinea. The invaders also wanted to destroy the naval resources that the guerrillas and the Guinean navy had in the port of Conakry, capture the leader of the party, Amílcar Cabral, and rescue a group of Portuguese soldiers held in a PAIGC prison. The incursion would not have the expected success concerning the insurgency and Portugal would be condemned by international organisations for the invasion of a sovereign state, but this operation would remain in the memory of many as the most daring carried out during the colonial war in Africa, although the Portuguese regime never acknowledged its involvement.[1]

The operation was the first of its kind carried out by Portugal and showed the capabilities of the elite black Portuguese troops, who managed to act far from their base of operations and return home safely. But the operation would not have the consequences foreseen for the course of the war, and even ended up benefiting Cabral's party in its struggle against the Portuguese forces. On the other hand, the operation also marked a change in General António de Spínola's strategy in Guinea. Appointed during the time of Salazar – the man who governed Portugal for three decades – to lead and command the Portuguese presence in the colony, Spínola tried to reverse the course of the war with a policy of social promotion of the populations combined with the neutralisation of the enemy abroad and the enticement of the guerrillas. By failing in Conakry, Spínola was convinced that the war had no military solution and that there was no other way but to negotiate with the PAIGC. Indeed, that is what he would try to do in 1972 with the mediation of the Senegalese president, Léopold Senghor, although without the success that Spínola wanted.

It is known that the official files relating to Operation Mar Verde were destroyed,[2] although there is some scattered documentation in the National Defence Archive in Paço de Arcos, Lisbon, and in the Central Library of the Navy – the Historical Archive (BCM-AH) in the COLOREDO-Guiné fund, in this case, declassified in 2016. This documentation was donated to the Navy archive in 1995 by the strategist behind the operation, Alpoim Calvão, but had already been disclosed by António Luís Marinho in *Operação Mar Verde – Um documento para a história* (*Operation Green Sea – A document for history*),[3] until now the most complete work published in Portuguese about this operation. There are also the testimonies of Alpoim Calvão and other protagonists in the RTP TV (Portuguese state broadcaster) series by Joaquim Furtado about the colonial war,[4] besides other interviews over time. Another important source is Calvão's book, published in 1976, which gives a direct testimony of the events under analysis.[5] The same is true of other works published by the Portuguese detainees who were in Conakry, such as Sergeant Lobato.[6] There are also several scattered articles on the subject, even a comic book by an ex-combatant, António Vassalo,[7] and finally a written statement by Spínola himself. As we will see below, there are also books by French-speaking authors dealing with the operation against Sékou Touré as part of the opposition movements against that African leader. What has been missing up until now is a work on the more remote background to the operation and its consequences on Spínola's strategy for Guinea. This is what is being attempted in this book, by framing Operation Green Sea in the period in which Spínola was in that territory.

It is clear that Mar Verde was a risky operation, not only politically but militarily. The political risk was high because the invasion of a border country could be condemned by the international community, further aggravating Portugal's isolation. The country had been subject to sanctions since the beginning of the war in Africa in 1961, and this invasion could have worsened the situation against Portugal. Furthermore, militarily it was not

The visit of Minister Silva Cunha to Guinea in 1970. Silva Cunha (centre) is accompanied by Spínola (to the left of the minister). (António de Spínola Collection)

guaranteed that a force of just over 300 men would be able to dominate the military and security forces of the neighbouring country, although Calvão was optimistic about this possibility. It was hoped that the elimination of Touré would lead to the success of the coup d'état and the installation of a government led by the regime's opponents, but to do so it was necessary to capture the Guinean leader and guarantee the security conditions necessary for the leaders of the opposition *Front de Libération National de la Guinée* (FLNG)[8] to seize power. Even so, it would be practically impossible not to associate Portugal with the coup, not least because there was the possibility of capturing Amílcar Cabral alive, which left Spínola with a massive problem on his hands: what to do with one of the most well-known guerrilla chiefs in Africa, who also held international prestige? Would Spínola be in a better position to negotiate a peaceful way out of the war with the leader of the nationalists, or would the guerrillas continue to fight? Or would the loss of support in Guinea-Conakry with the 'regime change' and the capture (or death) of Amílcar lead the guerrillas to give up the fight? Furthermore, how long would it be possible to maintain a government of the FLNG in Conakry, without external intervention and against the PAIGC and Cuban forces that were in the country? And what would be the reaction of the Guinean armed forces? Would they be faithful to the new power, or would they reject the government of the FLNG? These were questions to which there was no clear answer.

There is no doubt that the search for a political solution to the conflict, which would involve the integration of nationalists into colonial structures, was something that Spínola had been pursuing since 1970. Indeed, in one of his books written after the end of the war, Spínola states that "since the beginning of 1970 and with the knowledge of the Lisbon Government",[9] he had established the first contacts with the guerrilla leaders of the PAIGC and that "in those contacts, a plan was outlined which foresaw the transformation of the guerrilla forces of the PAIGC into African Units of the Portuguese Armed Forces and the appointment of Amílcar Cabral as Secretary General of the Province with the acting Secretary General,[10] as suggested and promulgated for that purpose". Although this was Spínola's intention, no direct contact was ever made with Amílcar Cabral to determine whether or not he would be interested in accepting his appointment to the post of Secretary General. This was confirmed by his brother, Luís Cabral,[11] when he labelled in his memoirs as "absolutely false any information seeking to make one believe that, directly or indirectly, there would have been official or unofficial contacts between the Portuguese Government or its representatives in Guinea and the management of the PAIGC."[12] Luís Cabral was also reported as saying that it was "crazy to think that an individual [such as] Amílcar … who was able to do all that fighting, could end up as Secretary General of the colonial government of Guinea. It is a complete absurdity."[13]

Silva Cunha,[14] who was Minister for Overseas Territories at the time, confirmed that during his visit to Guinea in March 1970 he met General Spínola, who was "euphoric at the results he had anticipated for the contacts he had made shortly before with the guerrilla leaders operating in the territory which, he said, would lead to the surrender and integration of the units he commanded into the Portuguese forces."[15]

It is undeniable that there were contacts, although at a lower level, and Luís Cabral confirmed them, although he said they were only of minor importance. However, Spínola convinced the authorities of the soundness of his plan, saying that in order to implement it "he went secretly to Lisbon to present his ideas to the President of the Council and the Minister of Overseas Territories, asking for (very large) funds, which were granted by the Minister of Finance, Dr João Rosas."[16]

It was in this context that the episode known as the 'death of the three majors' took place, with three senior officers of the Portuguese Army murdered in the Canchungo region. Spínola himself had established personal contact with a guerrilla chief, André Pedro Gomes, and had convinced himself that it was possible to bring an important group of guerrillas from the Canchungo area (then Teixeira Pinto) over to the Portuguese side. The three officers had meetings with the local guerrilla chiefs, but on 20 April 1970 (a month after Silva Cunha's visit to Guinea), when they went to receive the surrender of the guerrillas, they were assassinated.[17] General Spínola himself, who also went to the Canchungo area for talks with guerrilla leaders, probably only escaped the same fate as the majors thanks to the advice of the Secretary-General, Pedro Cardoso, who it appears persuaded him it was too dangerous to become involved in personal contacts with enemy leaders.[18] Spínola's gamble to lure the PAIGC in Chão Manjaco thus ended in tragedy.[19] Yet although the enticement of the guerrillas failed, Spínola was already preparing for Operation Green Sea, which in his opinion could radically change the course of the conflict.

The operation was prepared in great secrecy on the island of Soga, in the Bijagós archipelago. Curiously, an operation of such magnitude had been planned for several months without prior authorisation from the head of government, who only gave the green light to Mar Verde one week before it was executed. Despite the care taken in planning, Sékou Touré was suspicious of the movements of FLNG elements in neighbouring countries in search of support. The astonishment of Western nations, who knew nothing about the Portuguese plans, should also be noted. This can be seen in the case of France, which in the days following the invasion did not yet know whether the Portuguese were responsible for the military incursion.[20] The same can be said of the Federal Republic of Germany, which although being accused by Guinea's government of complicity with the Portuguese, knew nothing about the invasion.[21] The events in Conakry, however, were forever marked in the memory of many Guineans, not only by the surprise of the attack, but also by the repression the regime exercised over the alleged conspirators.[22] Accustomed to dealing with conspiracies – some real, others imaginary – Sékou Touré took the opportunity to rid himself of hundreds of internal opponents who were alleged to be involved in the attempted coup d'état. Many were arrested and others executed by order of a revolutionary court.[23]

The way in which the government reacted to the invasion has been portrayed in several works published in France, which give us a complementary insight into the events of 1970. Without seeking to be exhaustive, it is instructive to highlight the work of Bilguissa Diallo, daughter of a former Guinean dissident, Commander Thierno Ibrahima Diallo,[24] who participated in the attempt to overthrow the Sékou Touré regime and was wounded during the incursion.[25] In her book, Bilguissa Diallo analyses other works published in French which dealt with Conakry's invasion, as well as publishing documents which were in her father's possession. Another relevant but older work is that of Alpha-Abdoulaye Diallo – a former member of Touré's government and who played a number of roles in the government – which addresses the decisive moments of the operation in Conakry and the ensuing repression in which he himself was a victim along with many others. Diallo's work focuses on the period that the author spent in prison and the violence that the regime exercised over hundreds of people who were accused of complicity with the Portuguese, but also includes interesting details about the night of the invasion.[26] More recently, Pascal Airault and Jean-Pierre Bat have dealt with these events in a small book on undercover operations in Africa, but the authors draw on the book by Bilguissa Diallo and that of António Luís Marinho, bringing no new data to the subject.[27] It would have been interesting for the authors to research the French archives, a task I undertook in the archives of the French Ministry of Defence at Vincennes Castle in Paris, which revealed that the French knew nothing about the invasion, thus denying rumours of secret contacts between Alpoim Calvão and the French secret service. This ignorance is also evident in the German case. Adalbert Rittmüller, who was a diplomat in Conakry at the embassy of the Federal Republic of Germany at the time of the invasion, made a very interesting investigation in 2010 into how the West Germans were implicated in the plot against Sékou Touré through a very well conducted misinformation campaign by the East Germans.[28]

Also noteworthy is the very recent work of Carol Valade, Coralie Pierret and Laurent Correau, journalists from *Radio France Internationale*, who in 2018 published a series of articles on the origins and consequences of the operation in Conakry.[29] This work was part of a major investigation into the history of political violence in Guinea-Conakry, which the authors published that year.[30]

Finally, I would like to mention the work of Rui Hortelão, Luís Sanches de Baêna and Abel Melo e Sousa in their biography *Alpoim Calvão – Honra e Dever – Uma Quase Biografia* (*Alpoim Calvão – Honour and Duty – An Almost Biography*),[31] which refers to the preparations and execution of the operation and even gives some details about the contacts established with the FLNG representatives by Calvão himself in the final stage of the planning process.

Together, all these sources make it possible to reconstruct what was the bravest military operation ever carried out during the war in Africa, and which could have decided the course of the conflict in favour of Portuguese interests, although they also accentuate the international isolation to which Portugal was subjected. It is important too to place this operation within Spínola's overall strategy, which took great risks in sponsoring an attempted coup d'état in Guinea-Bissau's neighbouring country and whose failure made it impossible to eliminate the advantages that Cabral's party had in Guinea-Conakry. Spínola was thereafter convinced that there was no chance of reaching a military solution in Guinea and tried to find a negotiated solution that would pacify the colony.

1
Spínola in Guinea

When General António de Spínola was appointed in 1968 to command the Portuguese forces in Guinea-Bissau, the war was turning in favour of the PAIGC nationalists. Portugal was facing a colonial war on three fronts (in Guinea, Angola and Mozambique), but it was in Guinea that the Lisbon regime was most concerned. The PAIGC, led by Amílcar Cabral, had – with strong international support – successfully conducted a war of attrition against the Portuguese troops since 1963. The situation was known to the Portuguese government, which received information through military channels, but anyone who had access to the international press would also know what was happening in the small Portuguese colony.

In an article published in *The Washington Post* in 1968, a few months before Spínola's arrival in Guinea, Suzanne Cronje wrote the following:

> Unbiased witnesses say that more than half the rural areas of the territory are under the control of the PAIGC. The Portuguese are practically limited to fortified cities like Bafatá, and to isolated military garrisons that are supplied by helicopters. In recent months even the large urban centres have been attacked …
>
> The part of the territory under nationalist control is administratively run by Cabral. PAIGC has opened schools and hospitals in villages that have never before had such services. There is already a legislative and administrative organisation that has been favourably compared to that still run by Portugal …
>
> At the end of November, Prime Minister Salazar said that the terrorists did not control any part of Portuguese territory. This month the governor of Guinea-Bissau admitted that his authority did not extend to all parts of the territory.[1]

Salazar, who ruled Portugal under a dictatorship for over three decades, was certainly aware of what was going on, and naturally he was not very pleased with the conduct of the war in Guinea, having considered replacing General Arnaldo Schultz[2] as governor and military commander of the colony. Schultz had arrived in Guinea in 1964 but was powerless to contain the subversion that was spreading throughout the colony. Salazar is said to have been concerned after a visit to Guinea by the President of the Portuguese Republic, Américo Thomaz, in February 1968, who reported to him on his return that the country was on the brink of war.

Schultz was then recalled to Lisbon and removed from his posts, only returning to Bissau to bid his farewells.[3] Salazar then had to think of appointing an officer who could reverse the unfavourable situation in the colony. Spínola's name had been suggested for that role by the Defence and Overseas ministers, Gomes de Araújo[4] and Silva Cunha. Consequently, in May 1968, Salazar invited him to take up the posts of governor and chief commander of Guinea. The then brigadier had commanded a battalion in Angola at the beginning of the war in 1961 and had distinguished himself in that function as a military chief with a strong profile, but since then he had been vocal about the future of the Portuguese colonies in Africa.[5]

Amílcar Cabral had been the PAIGC's leader since the late 1950s. Although he was born in Guinea, his father was from the Cape Verde Islands. Cabral studied in Portugal, but from a young age he became an African nationalist, which led him to found the PAIGC. (Albert Grandolini Collection)

Portuguese President Américo Thomaz visits Guinea in February 1968. (Virgílio Teixeira Collection)

Spínola in Luanda, Angola, where he received the Medal of Military Valour for his actions in commanding troops. (António de Spínola Collection)

When he was called to the presence of Salazar, Spínola did not shy away from revealing his thoughts on the situation regarding the colonies, which did not exactly coincide with those of the President of the Council.

During the conversation, Salazar stressed that overseas territories were part of the Portuguese state and that the Portuguese forces had the capacity to confront the guerrillas; all that was needed was to wait for a change in the international situation to one that would be more favourable to Portuguese claims. However, he acknowledged that the case of Guinea was more complicated, as the Soviet Union was determined to make considerable efforts towards a favourable outcome to the guerrilla cause, which would then have serious consequences in both Angola and Mozambique. After listening to Salazar, the future governor of Guinea asked him if he could speak freely, and being granted permission he had the opportunity to set out his views on the overseas problem. Spínola felt that the colonies needed to be given more autonomy and a new overseas concept needed to be created to avoid international disputes. Spínola felt that the challenge facing Portugal would not go away and that to keep the colonies under Portuguese rule it was necessary to create a federative community (a multi-state nation), in which the member states would remain integrated because of the advantages they would have in being part of that community. To do this, Spínola stressed, a 'social revolution' had to be carried out which would benefit the local populations to the extent that they would desire to remain linked to Portugal and want to experience this policy in Guinea. However, to do so needed the support of the President of the Council. To Spínola's surprise, Salazar listened attentively without expressing the slightest disagreement, and concluded the conversation by telling him that it was urgent that he embark for Guinea.[6] A few days later, Spínola arrived in Guinea to take up his new post in place of General Schultz. He had inherited a rather serious political–military situation that required a new strategy to turn around Portuguese fortunes.

A new strategy

During his years in Guinea, Schultz had failed to contain the growing influence of the PAIGC, which held the military initiative, forcing the Portuguese forces into a defensive position.

The guerrilla activity extended to 60 percent of the territory and its combatants were better prepared for the irregular warfare in terms of weapons and organisation than the Portuguese troops they faced, which contributed to the growing spread of subversion.[7]

Moreover, the Portuguese military believed that they were clearly inferior to the guerrillas, a feeling that was negatively reflected in the state of mind of the forces deployed to defend the territory. The guerrillas also had the advantage of having their bases in neighbouring countries, where they could recover and reorganise their forces without being disturbed by Portuguese troops. Senegal and the Republic of Guinea were former French colonies, and both were ruled by African nationalists opposed to colonialism.

Senegal was governed by Léopold Senghor, a former member of the French National Assembly, who had become president when the country gained independence in 1960. Senghor had strong links to France, where he had studied and been a deputy, and was an advocate of the emancipation of African peoples, so it was only natural that he supported the independence of the

António de Oliveira Salazar was a Portuguese nationalist dictator who was President of the Council of Ministers from 1932 to 1968. It was during his time in office that the colonial war in Africa began. (via Albert Grandolini)

General Arnaldo Schultz during a visit to Porto Gole, Guinea, in February 1967. (José António Viegas Collection)

PAIGC guerrillas progress through a forest. The weapons they had were generally better than those of the Portuguese forces. (Albert Grandolini Collection)

Portuguese colony. As for the Republic of Guinea, it was governed by Sékou Touré, a former mayor of Conakry and also member of the French National Assembly. Touré had cut relations with France in 1958, when the country became independent, and aligned with the communist regimes of Eastern Europe, from where he received massive amounts of aid. Relations with the Soviet Union were strong, but Touré's government also had diplomatic relations with the US and some Western countries, such as Germany, from whom it received support through cooperation programmes.

Touré supported the PAIGC from the start of the armed struggle by providing logistical and military support. From the Republic of Guinea, the guerrillas infiltrated the colony's southern and eastern borders and maintained strong pressure on the border barracks. The situation in the colony was well summed up in a letter from the chief of Schultz's military cabinet, then Lieutenant Colonel Castelo Branco, who wrote: "The enemy puts his hand on our necks, like a good judo fighter, and we have difficulty in getting out of this position."[8]

When he arrived in Guinea, Spínola prepared an analysis of the current situation. An in-depth study on the military problem of Guinea included a map on the attitude of the population towards Portuguese colonial rule. In blue were areas in which the population recognised and obeyed the Portuguese authorities, while areas where the population was not exclusively loyal to either side were in yellow. In orange were areas where the population had abandoned their villages, pink showed areas controlled by the PAIGC, and areas where the population fled into the bush under guerrilla control were dashed. It can clearly be seen that the situation was not easy for the Portuguese forces, and that the guerrillas had infiltrated in several places in Guinea.[9]

Faced with this scenario, Spínola had to develop a new counter-subversion strategy in which the military dimension assumed a secondary role to a plan for economic and social development that guaranteed the well-being and progress of the populations in order to reduce the attraction of the insurgents. Spínola's opinion was that Portuguese troops should only be used only to guarantee security conditions and the time needed for this plan to be implemented. However, the armed forces would always be present in a counter-subversion capacity, as they appeared an indispensable condition to reduce the enemy threat and demonstrate the Portuguese military superiority to the people of Guinea.[10] In this way, the strategy defined was to combine military manoeuvring with an economic and social development plan capable of winning over the people and diminishing the influence of the PAIGC. Consequently, the war would be decided in the political-social field, although the guerrilla war had to be contained in order to allow the development of that policy. One region to which Spínola would give priority in the socio-economic field was the area known as the Chão Manjaco, in north-western Guinea, where he created a hospital and maternity clinic in Teixeira Pinto, health outposts in various localities and schools, as well as asphalting many roads.[11]

The guerrillas already had some groups in the area, commanded by André Gomes, and tried to develop their political–military implantation in the coastal areas of Chão Manjaco. Meanwhile, the guerrillas were also marking their position in some areas of the eastern sector, which in addition to the strong insurgency they already had in the southern sector of the colony, represented a gradual siege of the Bissau sector. To break this strategy, Spínola planned to act in Chão Manjaco by organising an attempt to lure the guerrillas to the Portuguese cause. He even met with the local guerrilla leaders in February 1970 with the aim of negotiating the surrender of the insurgents in Chão Manjaco.[12] A ceasefire was established in the region, but these contacts ended in tragedy in April with the death of the Portuguese majors who were leading attempts to lure the guerrillas. They were murdered on their way to a supposed meeting at which the guerrillas were going to turn themselves in. In spite of the failure of this enticement operation at Chão Manjaco, Spínola continued his policy of dividing the PAIGC by promoting internal divisions between Guineans and Cape Verdeans and by working with the ethnic groups that were more on the side of the Portuguese.[13] Indeed, Guinea was at this time a complex puzzle of ethnicities, with many rivalries, and the Portuguese exploited these to their advantage.

Leonid Brezhnev, who at the time was in the Presidium of the Supreme Soviet, visited the Republic of Guinea in 1961. (Albert Grandolini Collection)

Léopold Senghor and Sékou Touré, the presidents of Senegal and the Republic of Guinea, were the main African leaders supporting the PAIGC guerrillas. (Albert Grandolini Collection)

Another novelty in Spínola's policy was the people's congresses, which were aimed at winning the support of tribal communities by allowing them to express their concerns and interests in these spaces of debate. These congresses began in 1970 and had some success in Guinea by encouraging the civic participation of the various ethnic groups.[14] However, as pointed out by a well-known Portuguese official in the provincial government's propaganda structure, Otelo Saraiva de Carvalho, these congresses were only consultative and had no deliberative power, which created the false illusion that the indigenous people had some power of influence over the government authorities.[15] Furthermore, they were aimed at the populations already under Portuguese control, which excluded, from the outset, the ethnic groups that most supported the PAIGC.[16]

However, to succeed in this strategy, Guinea's new commander needed to reduce the guerrillas' military capacity, which required more combat resources and a higher level of operational ability. To solve the operational problem, Spínola would make a series of changes to the military structure that existed in Guinea, as well as increasing pressure on the officers commanding troops in the various units, which Spínola frequently visited.[17] As for the means, help was sought from Marcello Caetano, who in the meantime had replaced Salazar at the head of the Portuguese government

Leonid Brezhnev speaks to President Sékou Touré during his visit to Conakry in 1961. (Albert Grandolini Collection)

General Antonio de Spínola listens to local Guinean chiefs during a meeting in 1970. (DN)

Spínola speaking to some of the native population. He was usually well received by the Guineans. (Alvaro B. Geraldo Collection)

in September 1968. On 8 November, Spínola travelled to Lisbon for a meeting of the Supreme Council for National Defence (CSDN) and explained to Caetano and his ministers the situation facing him in Guinea. Spínola said that the situation was extremely critical, although some in the country were trying to hide the truth:

> Although I understand that, for obvious political reasons, it is important not to disclose the full gravity of the situation, I believe that the time has come for the Government of the Nation, which must decide in the interest of the National Whole, to become fully aware of the reality.
>
> And this is, unfortunately, quite different from the picture that emerges from some information produced in public which, aiming at political objectives of immediate reach, may harm the defence of the supreme and sacred interests of the Nation.[18]

In his presentation, the general reported that the PAIGC had about 5,000 combatants and that Portuguese forces numbered 25,000, although only 13,000 of those were combat forces. Nevertheless, the proportion of combatants was around 3:1 in favour of Portuguese forces, although Spínola considered that in a counter-insurgency war this proportion should be 5:1.

He also felt that the light armament the guerrillas had at their disposal was technically superior to that of the Portuguese troops, and that the PAIGC was receiving new types of armament – including RPG-7 rocket launchers, Czechoslovakian recoilless rifles and 120mm Soviet mortars (with a range of 5,700 metres) – that give it a superiority of fire over

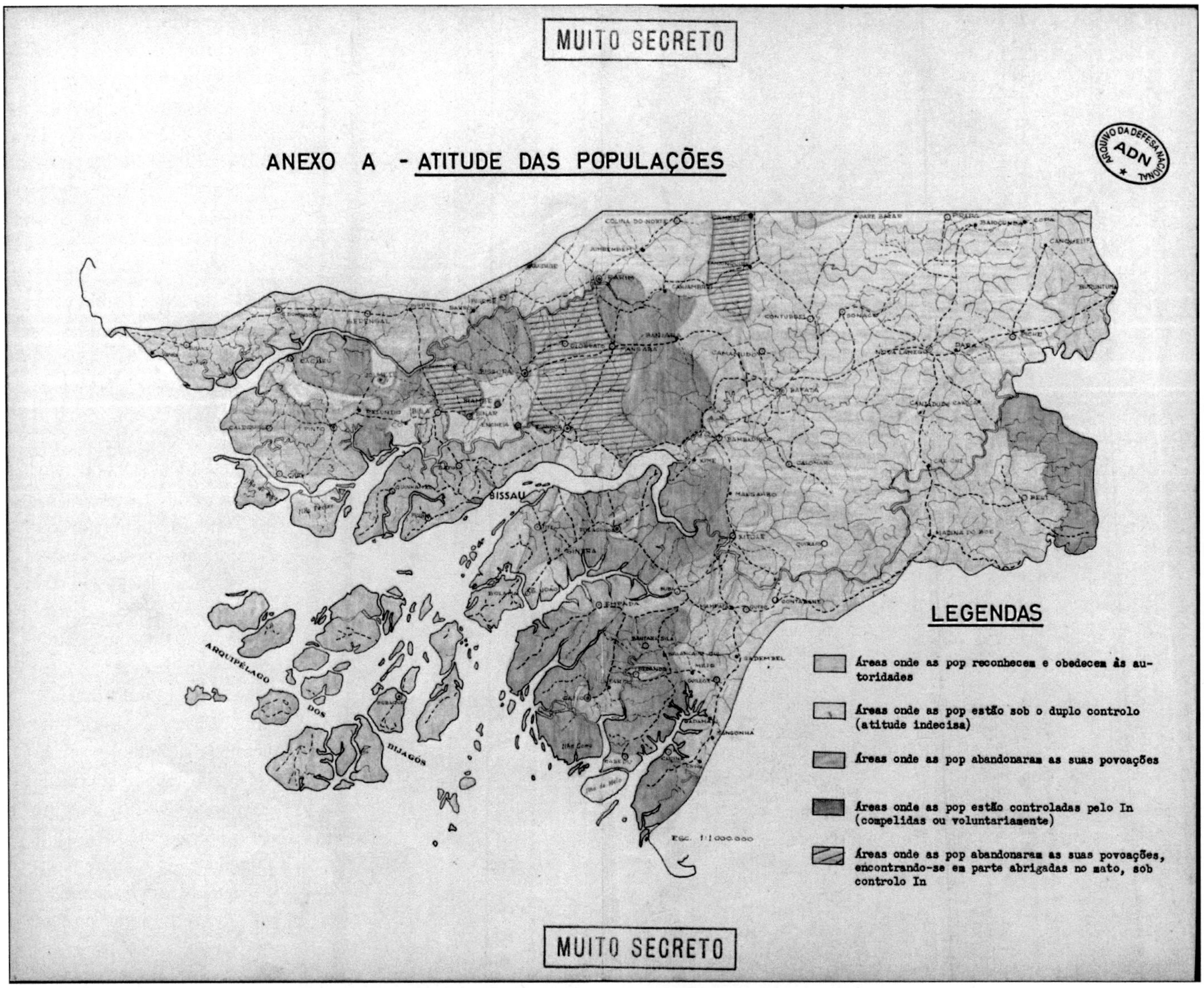

MUITO SECRETO

ANEXO A - ATITUDE DAS POPULAÇÕES

ARQUIPÉLAGO DOS BIJAGÓS

BISSAU

LEGENDAS

Áreas onde as pop reconhecem e obedecem às autoridades

Áreas onde as pop estão sob o duplo controlo (atitude indecisa)

Áreas onde as pop abandonaram as suas povoações

Áreas onde as pop estão controladas pelo In (compelidas ou voluntariamente)

Áreas onde as pop abandonaram as suas povoações, encontrando-se em parte abrigadas no mato, sob controlo In

MUITO SECRETO

Map of Guinea showing the attitude of the population towards Portuguese colonial rule. This map was drawn up in the context of a study on the military problem of Guinea made by Spínola in 1968. (National Defence Archive)

Commander André Gomes (seated) with two PAIGC fighters at a base in the interior of Guinea. André Gomes was the guerrilla commander in Chão Manjaco when Spínola tried to demobilise the guerrillas in this region in 1970. (via Albert Grandolini)

the reaction capacity of the Portuguese forces. The guerrillas also had anti-aircraft weapons in the border areas and had already shot down a Fiat G.91 fighter in July 1968 with a DShK 12.7mm machine gun.[19]

At this time, the Portuguese had several types of aircraft in Guinea. For combat missions they could use the Fiat G.91, which was the only jet fighter in Guinea, and the T-6 Texan, which although only a light aircraft could carry out some armed missions to support the troops. For transportation they had the Dornier Do 27 and Douglas C-47. They could also count on the Alouette III, a French helicopter that was very useful for the rapid

In certain areas of Guinea, the PAIGC was heavily infiltrated, providing basic services to the local population such as health and education. Seen here is a PAIGC cholera vaccination campaign. (Roel Coutinho Collection)

PAIGC fighters armed with AK-47s and a rocket launcher. (Albert Grandolini Collection)

A DShK 12.7mm machine gun captured by Portuguese troops. (National Defence Archive)

transport of troops and the evacuation of wounded personnel. This helicopter could also be armed with a 20mm cannon on the side door, and in this configuration was much feared by the guerrillas.

Airpower was the one great advantage that the Portuguese troops had over the guerrillas, due to their characteristics of firepower, range and manoeuvrability. Spínola also recognised that the guerrillas were well prepared for the six years of war, unlike the Portuguese troops, who could not compensate for their poor technical and tactical preparation for a counter-guerrilla war. In short, the PAIGC was better armed, more motivated and better acquainted with the territory where its members had always lived, having an increasing influence over the populations. To reverse this situation, Spínola hoped to obtain more human and material resources to implement a new counter-subversion plan, because in his view there was otherwise a risk of Portugal losing Guinea:

> Obviously, the current military situation in Guinea, where the negative mood of the combatant cadres is an influential factor, is critical and needs to be addressed by the Government, or the Nation will lose effective control of the Province and, consequently, its sovereignty over it.[20]

The possibility of losing the colony was not very well accepted by Caetano, who insisted at the meeting that the Portuguese presence was important in the territory for three reasons. Firstly, Portugal's enemies wanted to take control of Guinea; secondly, the defence of the colony was essential as moral support for the people living in Angola and Mozambique and the troops fighting in those southern territories; and thirdly, remaining in Guinea was essential to keep the archipelago of Cape Verde under Portuguese control, since the islands were of fundamental strategic importance for the dominance of the Atlantic and were therefore coveted by the Soviet Union. Consequently, Caetano pointed out, the Portuguese presence in Guinea was essential, not only for the defence of Portugal, but also for the West itself.[21] The meeting ended with Spínola stressing the urgency of the allocation of resources for his task:

> Mr Governor of Guinea again stressed that it is imperative to prevent the enemy from reaching the phase of military deployment throughout Guinea, otherwise our sovereignty will be irreparably lost. To this end, he urgently needs to be in a position, as he said in his presentation, to keep the remaining populations under proper control, which can only be achieved by allocating the requested reinforcements as a matter of great urgency.[22]

Alouette IIIs were used daily by the Portuguese forces to transport troops or evacuate wounded. (Albert Grandolini Collection)

In Guinea, the Alouette III was widely used in various missions. One of them was to transport Spínola on his frequent trips to visit troops outside Bissau. (Alvaro B. Geraldo Collection)

Spínola visiting a village in Guinea. In the background is a banner paying tribute to the governor. (Alvaro B. Geraldo Collection)

Spínola returned to Guinea in the hope that his requests would be met and that he would thus be able to contain the military capacity of the PAIGC and wrench the people from its control by developing an ambitious programme of social and economic promotion, with the slogan 'For a Better Guinea', all the while maintaining a strong military component.

In relation to this, he intended to develop a strategy based on several objectives, which included, above all, eliminating the replenishment lines of the guerrillas in the border areas while moving the populations most susceptible to the influence of the PAIGC to areas controlled by Portuguese forces and promoting their self-defence there. Spínola also aimed to retaliate against the border areas of neighbouring countries which were being used by the guerrillas to attack Guinea, and to set up mixed forces with Portuguese and African troops, with the recruitment of the latter to be expanded. Furthermore, the balance of power in the most vulnerable sectors of the territory was to be offset with the intervention of aviation, particularly in the so-called 'liberated areas' of the PAIGC.[23]

Lack of means

Despite Spínola's pleas, the reinforcement of resources for Guinea did not take place in due time, and in May 1969, during another visit to Lisbon, he handed the Chief of Staff of the Armed Forces (CEMGFA), General Venâncio Deslandes,[24] a further proposal for the strengthening of his hand. He complained about the lack of resources at various levels which did not allow the necessary military manoeuvres to be carried out, saying that the situation in the colony remained critical. In his letter, Spínola acknowledged the

Governor General Spínola visiting Guinea's interior by helicopter. (Alvaro B. Geraldo Collection)

Spínola in a native village. The general's strategy attempted to remove the native population from the PAIGC's influence. (Antonio de Spínola Collection)

Spínola during military operations in Guinea in 1968. The lack of means to carry out his aims was a common complaint of the general. (Alvaro B. Geraldo Collection)

understanding of Deslandes and the Minister of Defence over the urgent mobilisation of the means of reinforcement for Guinea, but at the same time considered that they were insufficient and represented only a minimal fraction of what he considered essential. The lack of a timely response from Lisbon meant that Spínola had to improvise solutions at a local level, without the government contributing to alleviating the situation.[25] The problem was also addressed at a meeting of the Council of Ministers on 19 May, at which Spínola was present. At the meeting, the Chief of Staff of the Army (CEME) reported that requests for overseas troops amounting to 26 battalions were very high in terms of costs and that the question of Guinea had to be analysed in this context. Spínola argued that the defence of Guinea should be made a priority, otherwise there was a risk of losing the colony. Caetano seems to have shared his thoughts, stressing the importance Guinea played in the overall defence of the overseas territories and agreeing that priority should be given to the war effort in that theatre of operations, to the detriment of Angola and Mozambique.[26]

It is clear from developments that some issues were to be resolved in 1970, particularly in the field of logistics,[27] but the government's difficulty in providing Spínola with the necessary resources due to budgetary constraints is still evident. The problems the Portuguese forces had in Guinea were basically common to other theatres of operations, where the troops found it difficult to cope with the guerrillas' movements due to a lack of resources. Spínola wanted special treatment with regard to his requests, as he

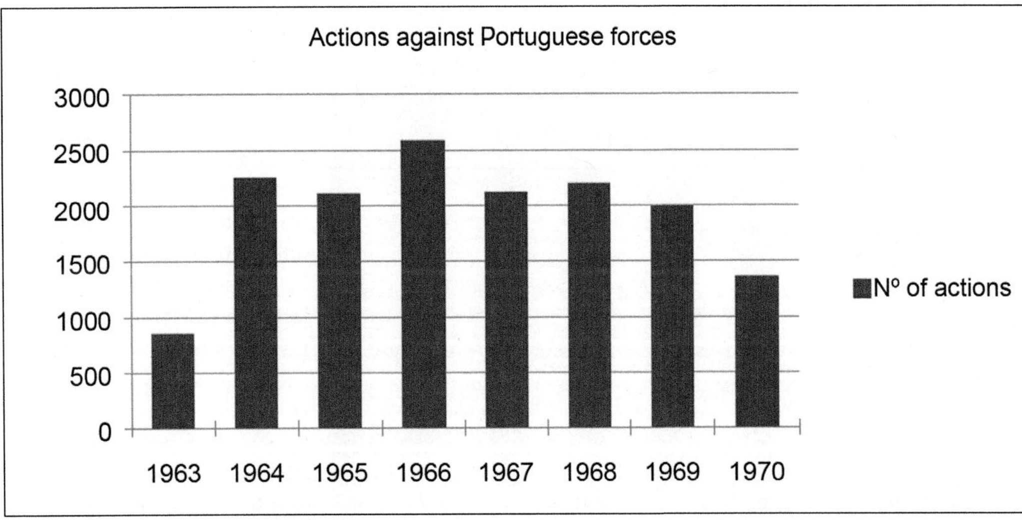

Chart 1: Actions against Portuguese forces

Amílcar Cabral with PAIGC fighters. (Fundação Amílcar Cabral)

with military force, convinced that the victory of the PAIGC only depended on improving its fighting and organisational capacity.[29] However, Aristides Pereira,[30] who was one of the PAIGC's most important leaders at this time, recognised that Spínola's social policy caused great problems for the guerrillas, who had no way of counterbalancing the aid that the people received. To reverse the situation, they had to ask for help from Sweden, which provided them with vital humanitarian support in the counter-campaign.[31]

In January 1970, the military command in Bissau carried out a study of the operational and logistical situation in the theatre of operations and the changes planned for 1970/71. The study estimated that the guerrillas had around 6,000 combatants, and that of these, 4,800 men would be engaged in operations within Guinea's territory. It said the PAIGC combat units (the so-called bi-groups) were well armed and trained, with Cuban military advisers specialising in combat, communications, explosives and health services.

Once again, a number of shortcomings affecting the Portuguese forces were pointed out in the study, in addition to the lack of prompt allocation of the reinforcements requested by Spínola, which could seriously compromise the strategy intended to combat the PAIGC and jeopardise the security of the native populations. It was estimated that the PAIGC's military capacity would gradually increase to 9,000 men in the regular guerrilla forces, and that the further evolution of the situation would depend on the Portuguese capacity to carry out the socio-economic programme aimed at the native populations and to halt the PAIGC's military offensive. There was also a fear that the guerrillas would be able to use air combat resources from a foreign power, launched from bases in neighbouring countries, namely the Republic of Guinea, which would affect the previous absolute air domination of the Portuguese Air Force (FAP, *Força Aérea Portuguesa*). To this end, anti-aircraft defences in Guinea, with radars and anti-aircraft artillery, would have to be reinforced, while a more efficient radar station and a French Mirage fighter squadron were also required. The Mirage issue would be a recurrent one in FAP requests, given that the Portuguese aerial branch had the ambition of deploying a supersonic fighter more capable than the Fiat G.91 and with the capacity to reach enemy territory in depth. However, the most serious prospect addressed in the study was that the PAIGC

felt that the situation in Guinea was more serious than in Angola and Mozambique. However, records show that a lack of resources was evident on all three fronts.

Despite Spínola's fears, the activity of the Guinean guerrillas in 1970 was at one of its lowest levels since the beginning of the war, being only higher than in 1963, which is significant, bearing in mind that the combat potential of the guerrillas has increased throughout the war. Chart 1 shows that the maximum peaks of activity took place during the Schultz period in Guinea, followed by a decrease when Spínola took over.

However, this decrease in guerrilla activity by about 30 percent compared to 1969 was not reflected in the number of casualties suffered by the Portuguese forces, which in 1970 reached a record of 890: 127 dead; 760 wounded; and three disappeared. The same is true of civilian casualties, with a record number of 1,174: 209 dead; 682 wounded; and 283 kidnapped. These figures clearly show an increase in the combat capacity of the PAIGC, which, despite committing fewer means, was able to obtain more success in its actions. This was most likely due to better training of its forces and a more careful choice of targets, which made it possible to obtain a better performance in the actions carried out.[28] In other words, the guerrillas responded to Spínola's psychological manoeuvring would be able to increase its numbers to 13,000 men (which it was believed could be possible from the end of 1972), which would trigger a final offensive on Portuguese troops and cause the collapse of the forces presently in Guinea.[32]

Meanwhile, on the ground, the situation remained unfavourable for Portuguese forces, which were often targeted by heavy artillery from neighbouring countries such as Senegal and Guinea-Conakry. Such provocations led Portuguese troops in November 1969 to attack the Samine base in Senegalese territory, from where the PAIGC launched artillery attacks on Portuguese positions in Guinea, which prompted a complaint by Senegal to the United Nations Security Council. In addition, the Senegalese government decided to send a reinforcement of troops (about 600 men) to the Casamansa region in the south of the country in order to guarantee border security at the border.[33] Dakar also intended to better control the movements of the PAIGC in Casamansa, but the guerrillas continued to move and attack positions in Guinea.[34]

A similar complaint had been made by Guinea-Conakry due to border incidents a year earlier. Given the repercussions of these complaints, the government in Lisbon ordered no further punitive incursions into neighbouring countries, thereby allowing the guerrillas so continue carrying out bombardments on the colony. The situation was then examined by the Portuguese Minister of Defence, Viana Rebelo,[35] at a meeting of the Supreme Council of National Defence on 30 January 1970:

> [T]he impossibility of retaliation by the NTs has led to a certain demoralisation and the Commander-in-Chief of the Guinean Armed Forces himself has repeatedly asked for permission to take such action: President Senghor's [Leopold Senghor, President of Senegal] repeated promises to effectively control the aggressive attitudes of PAIGC elements from Senegalese territory have not materialised, of course because the Senegalese Government has no power to do so.
>
> Against this background, the Minister for National Defence said it was imperative to take a firm stance, suggesting that he thought it would be best to make our reasons heard in the UN Security Council, so as to create conditions that could clearly justify any punitive actions that may be decided to be taken in relation to the countries that are allowing the current aggressions to our sovereignty.[36]

This position had already been expressed to Spínola in a letter dated 22 December 1969, in which Viana Rebelo asked the troops in Guinea not to return retaliatory fire on Senegal, although he recognised that this attitude implied "sacrifices and some demoralisation in the troops affected" when they could not fight back when fired upon.[37] Although at the January meeting he maintained the same position, the truth is that it opened the door to future punitive incursions into neighbouring countries, something that Spínola clearly advocated. A few months later, at the 24 July meeting of the Supreme Council, Rebelo said that Portuguese forces should only cross the northern border on occasional situations for the persecution of guerrillas who attacked Guinea and then sought refuge in Senegal. However, it was the opinion of those present that the relationship with Dakar should be preserved at all costs by avoiding problems with President Senghor, who was a great ally of the French in Africa and who seemed to be truly concerned about guerrilla actions from Senegal.[38] Indeed, Senghor tried to limit the facilities he had granted to the guerrillas in 1966, but continued to give his discreet support to Cabral's party. A different situation was that of Guinea-Conakry, where Sékou Touré openly supported the PAIGC, making that country the greater threat to Portuguese Guinea.[39]

Alpoim Calvão, who headed the Special Operations Department of the Commander in Chief in Guinea. (BCM-AH)

A radical solution

Spínola, of course, could not remain passive in the face of the facilities the guerrillas had in the neighbouring country. As early as 1968, in the context of military counter-manoeuvring, he had advocated "retaliatory action on the border areas of neighbouring countries, where the enemy would be supported in launching actions on national territory"[40]. But when he discovered that there was a movement of Guinean dissidents willing to overthrow Sékou Touré, he thought of a larger-scale operation to remove the dictator and install in Conakry a more moderate government favourable to Portuguese interests. Three weeks before the operation, on 1 November, Spínola wrote a letter to the Minister of Defence, Rebelo, warning of the daily worsening military situation and the concentration of guerrillas along the borders. To the north and north-east, Spínola estimated a concentration of around 2,500 PAIGC fighters, with around 1,500 on the southern border, supported by the regular army of the Republic of Guinea. The governor considered that the only way the PAIGC had to counter the success of his social strategy was by military force and that there was a risk of a dangerous escalation. Spínola did not have the means to counter this, complaining that "adequate solutions have not yet been found within the framework and at the level where the fundamental issues of a problem transcend Guinea", in a clear reference to the lack of political solutions to the war.[41] He continued:

> It is also clear that I will try in any case to avoid 'escalation', but in view of the imminence of a worsening of the situation in terms never before achieved in Guinea, or in any other Overseas

> Province, I can in no way rule out the adoption of measures projected on the border areas of neighbouring countries.[42]

Although the letter makes no reference to Mar Verde, Spínola was having difficulties in getting government support in Lisbon to carry out the operation. Indeed, the Minister for Overseas Territories had expressed his opposition to the operation by letter. Therefore, Spínola decided to appeal to Marcello Caetano directly. On 12 November 1970, he wrote him a letter in which he admitted that the PAIGC could win the war if its sanctuaries abroad were not neutralised, namely in the Republic of Guinea. In this regard, he asked for authorisation for an operation to be carried out in the neighbouring country with the aim of supporting a coup d'état led by armed and trained Guinean political dissidents in Guinea-Bissau.[43] Spínola was proposing a radical solution to resolve the war, which, if successful, could break the PAIGC's ability to continue to attack Guinea-Bissau and President Sékou Touré's ability to support Cabral's party. Spínola further requested that Caetano receive Alpoim Calvão, a special forces veteran, Commander of the Special Operations Department of the Commander in Chief, so that he could inform the head of the government of the chances of success of the planned action, which Spínola considered decisive for the outcome of the war in Guinea. On 13 November, Calvão went to Lisbon to speak with Caetano and was received by him on 16 November.[44] There is no official written account of their conversation, but according to Calvão, Caetano approved the operation (only a few days before it took place), insisting only that they leave no trace in Conakry that could compromise Portugal.[45] The most daring operation carried out during the colonial war, which Calvão had been planning for months, was thus authorised, although its origins went back even further, Calvão having wanted to deal with the situation since the previous year.

2
The Background to Green Sea

As we have seen, Spínola needed to neutralise the support that the PAIGC had in the Republic of Guinea in order to disrupt the guerrillas and control the military problem he had in Guinea. The best way to do this was to invade the neighbouring country and overthrow the Sékou Touré government, but such an operation was deemed too risky because of the repercussions it could have in the international community, although it would be highly rewarding if it succeeded.

We know that the idea of an incursion came to Alpoim Calvão in 1969 in the face of the realities in the theatre of operations.[1] In an interview[2] he explained:

> I started thinking about the Portuguese prisoners in Conakry, who by now were more than 20. They (the PAIGC) had faster boats than ours. Why didn't we go there and blow them up? I went to see the navy commander in chief, Commodore Luciano Bastos,[3] because General Spínola was in the Luso spa in Portugal. But the Commodore, agreeing with my suggestion, sent me to talk to Spínola. I got on a plane and went to Luso. My idea was to blow up the boats and bring the prisoners. Spínola agreed but asked me for a plan. I immediately started to prepare the plan. There was a group of opposition to Sékou Touré in contact with the Portuguese government.

This statement is consistent with the information contained in the official report on the preparation of the operation:

Amílcar Cabral and Sékou Touré. The leader of the Republic of Guinea was the major supporter of the PAIGC guerrillas. (INEP)

> As soon as the 'Nebula' operation was over, Commander Calvão embarked for the metropole [the parent state of the colony] in order to expose an idea to Governor General Spínola who was at the Luso spa. The idea was to eliminate the boats from the PAIGC [using limpet mines], at the main base itself, that is, Conakry.[4]

The PAIGC naval units had been listed since 1967 as probably P-6 class torpedo boats ('Project 183 Bolshevik'), although they lacked torpedo capacity due

The city of Conakry with the port in the background. (Albert Grandolini Collection)

to the absence of torpedo launch tubes. Thus, they were armed only with two twin 25mm AA cannon on the front and aft deck. Capable of reaching speeds over 40 knots, the P-6s were manned by Portuguese Guinea nationals trained in Russia, could quickly attack enemy vessels and could easily operate in coastal waters or rivers. In early 1968, the Portuguese Navy had already gathered much information about this small fleet of vessels. It was assumed that some were in the service of the PAIGC and that Cabral's party had sent about 50 individuals to the Soviet Union to train in the operation of these naval units. However, the Portuguese authorities did not know exactly what the PAIGC's intentions were regarding the use of these vessels. They could operate in the interior waters of Guinea with the aim of disturbing navigation on the River Cacine, in the south of Guinea, and thus affect the resupply of military units south of this river, or they could be employed in the Bijagós archipelago to interfere with ocean navigation in the access to Bissau through the River Geba channel. This river was the largest in Guinea, flowing into the Bijagós area, and it was through it that the maritime access to Bissau was made. However, both hypotheses were seen as unlikely (given the distances involved). Instead, it was felt most likely that the boats were being used for logistical links between the guerrilla bases in the Republic of Guinea and the PAIGC positions in the southern part of the colony. With regard to the Republic of Guine's naval resources, the Portuguese were convinced that they would only serve to patrol its territorial waters, and were not expected to be used in actions against neighbouring countries.[5]

All these naval means were sheltered in the port of Conakry, probably for fear of the Portuguese Navy or aviation, which could easily attack this type of shipping.[6] In addition, as we will see later, the training of the crews was deficient and their ability to operate their craft was not the best, so it is doubtful that they were capable of carrying out operations in the waters of the Portuguese colony.

Nevertheless, they were seen as a threat by the Portuguese and Calvão was willing to eliminate the PAIGC's naval forces with an operation in Conakry. Initially, the idea was to use a team of frogmen for a sabotage operation with limpet mines. This was the first idea of Calvão that received the agreement of Spínola and the Chief of the Navy, Vice-Admiral Armando de Reboredo. However, Portugal did not have these types of mines, but the South Africans did, so Calvão travelled there to negotiate for supply of the mines with the Bureau of State Security in Pretoria. Calvão was well received and returned with the mines on a commercial flight to Lisbon, thereby beginning preparations for the sabotage operation. For the operation to be successful, it was necessary for the Portuguese to update their information about the port of Conakry, so Calvão launched a night reconnaissance mission to the city using a Portuguese Navy boat, the LFG *Cassiopeia*, disguised as a PAIGC vessel. This mission was carried out on 17 September 1969 and Calvão was able to approach Conakry without any problems, successfully monitoring by radar a variety of details of the port, including the berthing jetties.[7]

But when Calvão returned to Bissau, Spínola presented him with another idea: why not carry out a larger-scale operation, taking advantage of the contacts with the anti-Sékou Touré opposition, which for several years had fuelled the idea of overthrowing the Stalinist regime in Conakry? That was how Operation Green Sea was born in Calvão's mind.

The dictatorship of Sékou Touré had led to dissent. Several groups of exiles had the intention of overthrowing the dictator, and naturally sought help from the Portuguese. The first contacts between the Portuguese authorities and Guinean dissidents on the possibility of military intervention in the Republic of Guinea took place in 1966. These contacts began in Guinea and involved requests for financial and material support or transit of military elements through the territory of the colony. One of the first contacts took place in mid-1966, when elements of the RGS (*Régroupement des Guinéans au Sénégal*, Group of Guineans in Senegal) contacted the Military Office of the Chief Command of Guinea to determine the possibilities and conditions of a collaboration with Portugal to overthrow the Sékou Touré government.[8] It was also in 1966 that the PIDE sub-delegation in Bissau (the political police of the regime, responsible for gathering intelligence) received the first requests for cooperation from the opposition FLNG.[9] These contacts were accompanied by General Arnaldo Schultz and the chief of the Military Office, Lieutenant Colonel Castelo Branco, but in Lisbon there were great reservations as to the real capacity for action of these opposition movements, and it was decided not to give aid to any of them. The FNLG's plan was to launch guerrilla and sabotage actions from Guinea-Bissau against the neighbouring country, but this idea was abandoned in Spínola's time because of the risk of international condemnation, which it was feared could even lead to armed intervention in favour of Sékou Touré.

The situation as it stood can thus be systematised as follows:

a) When Alpoim Calvão proposed the operation to destroy PAIGC boats and recover the Portuguese prisoners in Conakry, there were already contacts between Sékou Touré's opponents and the Portuguese government, about which he was informed by General Spínola.
b) According to existing documentation, the idea of forming a guerrilla movement from Guinea to attack Guinea-Conakry was even considered, but the idea was abandoned because of the risks of condemnation by the international community.
c) The establishment in Conakry of a government more favourable to Portuguese interests meant ending the presence of the PAIGC in that country, which would be extremely important in changing the military and political situation in Guinea-Bissau. Moreover, as we will see, in a document delivered to the Portuguese government by a qualified representative of the FLNG, the intention to put an end to the activities of the PAIGC in Guinea-Conakry was clearly expressed.

Spínola himself commented in a statement he made after the war:[10]

> The operation had two objectives: the first, of a high strategy and an external nature, with a view to supporting a coup d'état in the Republic of Guinea; the second, of an internal nature, aimed at dismantling the PAIGC facilities in Conakry, imprisoning Amílcar Cabral and releasing the Portuguese military held in PAIGC prisons [...]. The death of Amílcar Cabral was forbidden and he was to be imprisoned and taken to Bissau,[11] where his presence was a key factor in my manoeuvre to conduct the political-military process under way in Guinea, with a view to a 'ceasefire' that I considered highly honourable for Portugal.[12]

We can see from Spínola's testimony that the operation had several important strategic objectives that could radically change the war, leading to a ceasefire and Cabral's imprisonment in Bissau, leaving the guerrillas without leadership. However, for everything to work it was essential that the FLNG was prepared to take power in Conakry, and although that was its intention, the negotiations with the Ministry for Overseas Territories in Lisbon were not promising. Although contacts were maintained, the Portuguese avoided committing themselves to any operation. These reservations were caused by a lack of confidence in the FLNG, which was felt to be too weak to be able to carry out a successful operation against Sékou Touré. Even so, the Guineans did not give up; they kept in contact with the Portuguese authorities in a bid to receive support for their actions and try to convince the Portuguese of their good intentions. As we will see later, these contacts went through Switzerland, where a leading FLNG member worked. Around 1968, these contacts were regular and there was great pressure from the FLNG for the Portuguese government to finance an operation against Sékou Touré.

FLNG's intentions

Indeed, on 28 June 1968, Alexandre Ribeiro da Cunha[13] signed, under the letterhead of the Office of the Minister for Overseas Territories, a 'Top Secret' document[14] in which he stated that he had been:

> [S]ought on 24 June in Geneva by Mr Doré, an official of the BIT (*Bureau International du Travail*) and a national of the Republic of Guinea (who is already known in Lisbon) who wished to introduce me to the head of his movement and, if that movement was successful, the future President of the Republic of Guinea. After all, we were old and good friends! This is David Soumah,[15] General Secretary of the Trade Union Confederation whom I have known for many years … . Given my 'intimacy' with Soumah, Doré opened up completely.

The document goes on to report on the information given about the intentions of the FLNG:

> They have everything planned to take down Sékou Touré. To do so, as they have already said in Lisbon, they need the agreement of Portugal. According to Soumah, the plan would be implemented as follows:
>
> On the occasion of a public demonstration, one group would create confusion and two other groups, previously infiltrated, would neutralise the Cuban camp and occupy the radio [station]. They are sure [that] the elites and the population would accompany them and that one day they would become masters of power; Soumah knows that all the religious and tribal leaders accompany him. The army is also with them except the Cubans (about 250 men) and a few Chinese police instructors.
>
> Their movement has the support of Côte d'Ivoire and Senegal does not pursue it because it would like them to achieve their objective.
>
> They need Portuguese support, not for our territory to break the 'infiltration' but for the preparation and meeting of the groups that will infiltrate. The main base would be in Sierra Leone. To my question about the support of this country, they answered that in Sierra Leone everything is about money. They know that with £2,000 they will buy the commander of the

military camp near the border who will be the first to lead them to infiltrate.

They would like the plan to be examined by the Portuguese authorities who could give their advice. They could come to Lisbon between 10 and 15 July next.

Until 12 July there was no reply, but on that date Ribeiro da Cunha stated that Doré had phoned him from Geneva to inform him that David Soumah would be there from the 13th to the 15th of that month and "wanted to know if he could come to Lisbon for the purposes mentioned in the previous note",[16] adding that both wanted to come to Lisbon "as urgently as possible".

There does not seem to have been a response, because on 11 August new information came from Ribeiro da Cunha, again under the letterhead of the Ministry of Overseas Territories and classified as 'Top Secret':

At 1.30 p.m. on August 10, Mr Doré spoke again about Genève. He wanted to know if Mr Camará had spoken to me. I answered in the affirmative and, to a question from Mr Doré, I simply answered that he had spoken to the appropriate people.

Mr Doré told me that Mr David Soumah had called him from Dakar saying that everything was ready and that the best time for the initiative would be in the first half of September. And he ended with the sentence: '*Nous comptons sur vous*' [We are counting on you].[17]

In fact, Camará Boubacar had already been received by one of the "appropriate people", but apparently the FLNG's proposal had not aroused much enthusiasm. There are two pieces of information on the subject, both typed and dated 8 August but not signed.[18] The first recorded:

Asked about the means available to his 'movement' to achieve the plans he has in mind, he said he had men trained in Côte d'Ivoire, from where they would leave in 'H hour', framed by French military technicians that the French government agreed to provide them, and he added that from Côte d'Ivoire they would move to Liberia, Sierra Leone and Conakry.

He also said that, with the independence celebrations taking place on 28 September and the 'artistic week' beginning on 10 September, with the presence of numerous artists from various African countries, they decided to take advantage of this festive hour to launch the coup.

Asked what they could offer in return for possible aid from the Portuguese authorities, he replied: 'The immediate establishment of diplomatic relations with Portugal and the liquidation of the PAIGC.'

This information is followed by a 'comment' on the same page, also typed:

As a personal opinion and in addition to the aid requested (which would not be too much if the plan worked) it seems to me that the 'movement' will lack structures capable of making it a success.

At the top, handwritten and also dated 8 August, with an unreadable rubric, is the following:

Doré, who wrote the letter to Dr. Rib°. da Cunha, seems to have spoken to Dr. Hall Themido in the case. Dr. Caldeira Coelho[19] was going to speak to Mr. M° N. E. about it today. Boubacar returns today to the PIDE and we will try to find out what they count on for the action.

The second piece of information, also typed and unsigned, has the same date as the previous one. It is apparently a continuation of the first, although more detailed:

Following a conversation with the Guinean Camará Boubacar, the following points were clarified: 1 – The means available to them in men and arms; 2 – The elements they have in the interior of the Republic of Guinea; 3 – The possibility of support from the Government of France, Côte d'Ivoire, Sierra Leone and Senegal.

On these points he said: 1 – In Côte d'Ivoire, Senegal and Sierra Leone there are about 1,100 men, former Guinean members of the French army, who have neither weapons nor means of transport, which they expect to obtain if they get our financial aid. 2 – He said they have some ministers and former ministers, army officers and leaders of '*Jeunesse*'. 3rd – From French support, he can only indicate that the Ivorian government has made contact with the French government with a view to overthrowing the Sékou Touré regime, assuming it has his support; he does not, however, give any concrete data.[20]

Sierra Leone, Senegal and Côte d'Ivoire have allowed and permit the presence of members of the 'FLNG – National Liberation Front of Guinea' and their transit for action on Guinean territory.

Nothing could be clarified about financial and war material support.

The comment of the writer is frankly pessimistic:

It seems to us that the aid we are being asked to provide resembles a lottery game but, nevertheless, Camará Boubacar has been asked to draw up a report focusing on these matters, which it has to do and deliver tomorrow.

The promise seems to have been kept, as indicated by an extensive handwritten document in French entitled 'Note to the attention of the competent Portuguese authorities', dated Lisbon, 9 August 1968.[21]

This 'Note' – after outlining the formation of the FLNG[22] and detailing the support received, particularly from Côte d'Ivoire, the organisation of the movement and the internal difficulties themselves – states that there are "clandestine subsections" within Guinea-Conakry and support from politicians and members of the Guinean Army General Staff. They also had about "1,500" military personnel, former combatants of the French Army, scattered throughout the Ivory Coast, Senegal and Sierra Leone, of whom "300 have been trained for about a month", with a view to being used in "the action which we are facing for the first fortnight of September 1968, on the occasion of the artistic fortnight which each year precedes the celebrations marking the anniversary of independence".

Regarding the mission that had gone to Portugal at the time, it is stated that its "objective is to obtain from the authorities of Portugal, which we consider as natural allies of our just fight, a material and financial aid, the details of which are in a document attached to this note".

If agreement is reached, the document continues:

> [T]he commitments that the FLNG makes with regard to Portugal are as follows: systematic liquidation of the PAIGC and all its bases on the territory of the Republic of Guinea; total neutralisation of the border common to our two countries; diplomatic recognition of Portugal; opening of a consulate in Lisbon; establishment of trade relations.

Camará Boubacar's note expresses the conviction that "all the conditions for a coup d'état in Guinea are now in place" and explains in more detail the support available to the FLNG on other occasions. In Côte d'Ivoire, where "300,000 Guineans" live, the movement is officially recognised; in Senegal, "it maintains good relations with President Senghor ... the organisation functions normally, without any limitations and our leaders travel with Senegalese passports"; in Sierra Leone, "our relations with the previous military government were excellent but the sudden changes in recent months have put us in a position of expectation *vis-à-vis* the authorities", although close contacts had been established between the two parties because "from a strategic point of view, Sierra Leone deserves our particular attention because it is from its borders that all operations directed against Conakry will depart". As for France, with whose government the FLNG had apparently never had direct contact, it appears that there was a trace of union between that country and Côte d'Ivoire. "We are convinced," he continued, "that the support, freedom and security enjoyed by the movement and its members in the two French-speaking countries mentioned above is in part the result of the very discreet action of the French authorities."[23]

The following information can be extracted from the document:

1) Boubacar places great emphasis on Guinea-Conakry's future good relations with France, which he says "has been aware of our military preparations since January 1968" and asserts that "French officers have regularly maintained and are in contact with us" which "means that France is interested".
2) He protests that the FLNG does not intend to organise a guerrilla war but to launch a "rapid command action against the person of Sékou and some of his lieutenants immediately followed by a major operation to neutralise the situation".
3) He also reaffirms that "in addition to all the people, who are heart and soul with us, several battalions of the armed forces have been won for our cause, including numerous cadres of the State".

Finally, the concrete request for the support to be received from Portugal emerges:

> The only urgent and very important problems are: the material we ask from Portugal and [...] 40,000 Francs, or 160,000 dollars to guarantee the transport of the men and their maintenance during the campaign in the special conditions prevailing in this region.

In addition to the money – equivalent, at the time, to less than 5,000 escudos – the materiel requested for the 300 former soldiers was "180 rifles, 60 machine guns, 30 automatic pistols, 30 grenade launchers, six machine guns, 300 daggers", as well as "the ammunition for these weapons, a certain amount of offensive, defensive, incendiary grenades, petards and mines" and "a complete pharmacy, if possible". The delivery of the equipment, on a date to be agreed, would take place "in the Gambia or on the high seas, with the help of a fishing boat which we will charter for that purpose".[24] On 29 August there was a new letter from Doré to Ribeiro da Cunha, seeking to know if there was any decision by the Portuguese government, with a note from the latter, dated 2 September, informing the minister about this new step.[25]

The involvement of PIDE

From reading all these various documents, it can be seen that neither the Ministry of Foreign Affairs nor the Ministry of Overseas Territories[26] shared the FLNG's enthusiasm for Portugal's participation in an attack on Guinea-Conakry, and that they even had great reservations about the support that Portugal should give. These reservations are evident from a note to the Chief of Staff of the Armed Forces from the Director General of Political Affairs of the Ministry of Foreign Affairs. In this document, dated 17 January 1969 and signed by Caldeira Coelho, a note is attached of a conversation between Jean Marie Doré and a Portuguese diplomat, Leonardo Mathias, on the possibility of military intervention in the Republic of Guinea. Caldeira Coelho said in the document:

> [A]part from good wishes and intentions, Mr Doré does not count on any elements and hopes that these will be provided, practically in their entirety, by Portugal, which we will not be able to do and that is not Portuguese policy. It also seems that there is a need to ensure that someone close to President Sékou Touré, on his behalf, has infiltrated Mr Doré's movement in order to seek evidence against Portugal. In these circumstances, no action will be taken on the suggestions and requests of the person concerned, to whom only their views will be considered.[27]

Faced with this opinion, one is obviously led to ask what happened in the following months in order for the FLNG project to gain support, and which entity, or entities, supported the idea? We note, from a certain moment, the involvement of the PIDE political police, since a document refers to a meeting in Geneva on 6 and 7 December 1969 with David Soumah and Jean Marie Doré, at which the PIDE was present. At this meeting, the leaders of the FLNG once again asked for the support of Portugal, not only financially (3,500 contos – $120,000) but also logistically to train about 100 men in Guinea who would then participate in the operation. The PIDE members considered that the FLNG presented "an organisation and structures likely to achieve its objectives. On the other hand, in the field of information, they are able to provide us with valuable elements that can help us a great deal in the war that we are waging against the PAIGC in the Overseas Province of Guinea." According to the PIDE, the final objective would be the elimination of both Sékou Touré and the PAIGC.[28]

According to José Freire Antunes, a Portuguese historian who devoted great attention to the colonial war, the direct contact in the PIDE was the Deputy Director General and head of the African department of the political police, Inspector Barbieri Cardoso.[29] Inspector Cardoso was the one who handed the supplier the cheque for $2,450,000 to pay for the purchase of the weapons that were used in the operation, including 250 Kalashnikovs, 20 mortars and 12 RPG-7 grenade launchers, which shows the deep involvement of the political police in the preparations for the incursion in Conakry.[30]

This involvement would also be evident in Bissau from the close collaboration between Calvão and the chief of the political police in Guinea, Deputy Inspector Matos Rodrigues, although the PIDE/DGS delegation then failed in what it was expected to do: provide correct information for the movement of the invading forces.[31] The PIDE (and then the DGS, which succeeded it in March 1969) maintained an intelligence-gathering service in the Republic of Guinea practically from the country's independence. This information was sent to the Presidency of the Council, the Ministry of National Defence, the Ministry of Overseas Territories, the Ministry of Foreign Affairs and, of course, the Commander in Chief of Guinea. In addition to details of the border movements, the PAIGC guerrillas, the military and even the people of the Republic of Guinea were given information on the political and social instability of Guinea-Conakry and on external threats, which – coinciding with what the FLNG claimed – was such as to convince the Portuguese authorities of the fragility of Sékou Touré's position. For example, on 11 June 1969, a report said there were "movements on the border of the Republic of Guinea with Côte d'Ivoire because Sékou Touré feared any action by the FLNG in those areas". Then on 17 June 1969, further information assured that "the Guinean authorities have stepped up surveillance on the Buruntuma border because they are waiting for a group of former French fighters who are enemies of Sékou Touré to infiltrate from Paris to help the opposition plotters who are imprisoned in Conakry".[32]

Sometimes there was some inaccuracy in what was said, as for example in a report of 18 March 1969[33] in which it was stated that the internal situation in Guinea-Conakry was still "tense". The report added: "After the failed coup against Sékou Touré relatively recently, this president stopped staying at the Government Palace and did so in the district of 'Belle Vie'[34] [*sic*] in the northern part of that capital, which is about 8 kilometres from the Palace." Here one can ask what is meant by "relatively recently" and whether the information that Sékou Touré had spent the night in that residence was not confirmed until November 1970, leading the invading forces to destroy it.[35]

There is no doubt that Spínola was deeply involved in the plan, going beyond the proposal to release the prisoners and destroy the speedboats. Initially, the general thought of installing an FLNG guerrilla movement in Guinea, capable of carrying out actions in the Republic of Guinea, but this goal was later abandoned in favour of the coup d'état.[36]

In October, when preparations for the operation were well advanced, Calvão himself went several times to Geneva and Paris, almost always accompanied by Deputy Inspector Matos Rodrigues of the DGS,[37] in order to establish contacts with representatives of the FLNG, such as Jean Marie Doré, who was collecting funds for the operation, David Soumah and Thierno Diallo, a former French Army officer who would lead the movement's military committee. At the same time, agreements were established between the Portuguese government and the Front. These agreements were intended to remain in force after the coup had been consolidated and provide, among other things, for the banning of the PAIGC in the Republic of Guinea. Subsequently, three representatives of the dissidents in Guinea-Conakry even settled in Bissau, having drawn up a list of potential future rulers and drafted declarations and proclamations. However, a report[38] signed by David Soumah reveals that the decisive meetings to implement support for the FLNG took place in Lisbon: "[A]fter two meetings in Lisbon, it was from 21 December 1969 that operations [in support of the FLNG] were effectively initiated. A first payment of $50,000 was earmarked for the establishment of three committees and their operation: 1) Political committee 2) Information committee 3) Military committee, as well as networking in Senegal, the Gambia, Sierra Leone, Guinea and Mali." According to this document, these structures were set up in January and February 1970. The report also states that the political committee was operating in Dakar, where Soumah was, and was the coordinating centre with links to Geneva and Lisbon. Due to a disagreement with Soumah, Thierno Diallo did not appear as the leader of the military committee, nor in its composition; however, the military committee was in charge of recruiting Guineans in Senegal and Sierra Leone, as well as paying them. According to Soumah, recruitment had begun in May 1970 with small groups so as not to attract the attention of the Guinean embassy in Dakar, but Calvão insisted on recruiting larger groups until a serious problem arose: Thierno Diallo was arrested in Senegal while recruiting a group in the Kolda region.[39] The arrest came to the attention of the regime in Conakry, which asked for his extradition, but his wife – together with the writer Camara Laye[40] – managed to convince the French Ambassador in Senegal to ask for the prisoner's deportation to France, since Diallo was a former French officer living in Dakar. Consequently, he escaped extradition and was sent back to Paris.[41]

Complicities

Although the arrest of Diallo was a sign that Senegal did not tolerate certain activities on its territory, the truth is that the two main leaders of the FLNG (Doré and Soumah) had privileged contacts with President Senghor, of whom Doré was a personal friend. At a meeting in Dakar on 19 March 1970, Doré and Soumah reportedly told the Senegalese leader that they were ready to act against Sékou Touré, with Senghor saying that they could count on his understanding "to act as and when they understood as long as they did not create diplomatic problems for him, and even suggested that they should not hesitate to ask the Portuguese government for help".[42]

The same was true for President Felix Houphouët-Boigny of Côte d'Ivoire. Being a moderate political leader, he was anti-communist and had no sympathy for Sékou Touré. Knowing this, it was with Houphouët-Boigny that Diallo would also seek support (before his arrest in Senegal) by travelling to Abidjan to meet him. Diallo was well received by the president, who was receptive to supplying arms to the FLNG.[43] It was thus clear that both Senegal and Côte d'Ivoire supported the overthrow of Sékou Touré, although publicly they could not admit such a stance. The FLNG was also active in other countries such as the Gambia, where in October 1970 a group of 38 Guineans was sentenced by a court on charges of organising an expedition to overthrow Sékou Touré. The group had been arrested near the Senegalese border as they were preparing to embark on a Portuguese boat for Guinea-Bissau.[44]

However, given the favourable situation he foresaw, Spínola went ahead with preparations for the coup, which, if it succeeded, would be of the utmost importance for Guinea-Bissau. This is clearly shown by the letter already referred to in the previous

President Senghor (right, in suit) and Sékou Touré (centre, in suit and hat). Senghor obviously knew of the Portuguese plans to invade Conakry. (Albert Grandolini Collection)

chapter addressed to Marcello Caetano on 12 November 1970,[45] a week before the Mar Verde operation, in which he wrote:

> In view of the reservations expressed in the last letter I received from the Minister for Overseas Territories, I have taken the liberty of sending Lieutenant Captain Guilherme Alpoim Calvão, Head of the Special Operations Department of the Command-Chief, to the metropole with the task of documenting the possibility of success in the planned action, which I have no doubt will be decisive for the outcome of the war in Guinea. For my part, I assume full local responsibility for its launch, taking the necessary risks, as I remain firmly convinced that, despite the indisputable successes already achieved in the context of a social counter-revolution, we will lose Guinea irreparably if we do not neutralise the enemy abroad.

Alpoim Calvão was received by Caetano on Monday, 16 November, having received authorisation from the President of the Council to proceed with the invasion, agreeing with that officer that the release of Portuguese prisoners would be enough for the operation to be considered a success.

The situation at this point can be summarised as follows:

1) Calvão's first idea for an operation in Conakry essentially had two initial objectives:
- destroy the PAIGC boats in a sabotage operation;
- release the Portuguese prisoners.

2) When Calvão revealed this action to Spínola, the latter agreed and informed Calvão that there were contacts between the Portuguese government and Sékou Touré's opponents, and that these elements could be used to set up a military branch of the FLNG in Guinea and unleash guerrilla actions against the neighbouring country. This idea was then abandoned in favour of a larger-scale operation to overthrow the dictator and also free the Portuguese prisoners who were being held in Conakry.

3) These contacts had been taking place since 1966 and were aimed at obtaining Portugal's support for the invasion of Guinea-Conakry, an operation that would be carried out exclusively by nationals of that country. The support requested was limited to a minor financial contribution to the training of FLNG elements and the supply of duly specified military materiel. In return for this support, the FLNG would ban the activities of the PAIGC on the territory of Guinea-Conakry, at least as long as the new government of the Republic of Guinea remained in power.

4) António de Spínola not only knew about the talks between the Portuguese government and the FLNG, but he was always institutionally aware of the PIDE's contacts with the FLNG, which – even if there were no other evidence – is confirmed by two official telegrams addressed by Minister Silva Cunha to the Governor and Commander-in-Chief of Guinea, signed simply, as was customary, 'Minister'. One of these telegrams, dated 14 October 1969, says that "Doré telephoned saying David[46] is waiting for indications from Matos Rodrigues"; the second message, ten days later, on 24 October, says: "Doré telephoned yesterday from Geneve informing that he had received a communication from Mamadou. He followed up on his request and warned David."[47]

As already stated, and Alpoim Calvão confirmed, both the Minister for Overseas Territories and the Minister for National Defence – as well as the Ministry for Foreign Affairs – "disagreed with the project for fear of the international repercussions".[48] However, the operation only came to fruition much later, in a completely different form and apparently at a higher material cost than that required to satisfy what the FLNG had initially requested. The idea of creating a guerrilla movement from Guinea-Bissau or Sierra Leone was abandoned for fear of the international repercussions this might have caused, and the initial objectives proposed by Commander Calvão were considerably expanded: the action against the PAIGC boats turned into support for a coup d'état, led from Portuguese Guinea territory, with Portuguese military and African commandos, who were, or at least were accompanied by, Guinean citizens gathered in neighbouring countries and trained in Guinea-Bissau. The operation's aims now included 'neutralising' Sékou Touré, occupying the radio station, destroying the motor torpedo boats in the port of Conakry and the MiG fighters of the Guinean Air Force, and dominating the presidential forces: the republican guard, militias and gendarmes.

Spínola, perhaps lacking confidence in the military capacity of the Guineans to bring the invasion to a successful conclusion on their own, but enthusiastic about the possibility of ending the presence of the PAIGC in Guinea-Conakry, convinced Marcello Caetano to authorise the operation with the participation of Portuguese forces and from the Portuguese colony. Consequently, a detachment of special marines made up of Guineans and a company of African commandos were involved in the operation. However, the ultimate failure of the operation had serious consequences. Firstly, it would lead to the consolidation of the Touré regime in Guinea, which took the opportunity to kill many of its potential opponents – some hanged on the bridges of the capital, for example, with others thrown into prison, where they would die or would remain so long as Touré lived. Furthermore, in December 1970, in response to a request for help from the Guinean chief of state, the Soviets sent a naval force with two ships, one of which was armed with missiles, to the waters off Guinea, to which an amphibious ship would later be added.[49]

3
The Invasion of Conakry

The attack on Conakry was prepared in great secrecy on the island of Soga, in the Bijagós archipelago, away from indiscreet eyes. It was on this isolated island that about 200 Guinean exiles were trained for the operation. Alpoim Calvão was in charge of collecting the Guinean dissidents, who were recruited by the FLNG in African countries such as Senegal, Sierra Leone, Côte d'Ivoire and the Gambia, where many of them were in exile. In the first months of 1970, more than 100 Guineans were recruited in Africa and taken by night in Portuguese boats to the island of Soga.[1] These exiles were recruited by local FLNG leaders, who paid them a sum of money and then organised their collection by Portuguese boats, which were not typical ones for this type of operation. The LFG *Orion* commanded by Commander Faria dos Santos was used several times in these covert recruitment operations.[2] At the same time as the Guineans were preparing for the invasion, information about the capital of the Republic of Guinea, Conakry, about which the Portuguese knew very little, was also being collected.

Calvão had already carried out a night reconnaissance mission to the port of Conakry in September 1969 with LFG *Cassiopeia*,[3] as previously mentioned, to prepare a sabotage operation with limpet mines. However, this plan was subsequently abandoned in favour of Operation Mar Verde. Up-to-date maps of the city were lacking and the Portuguese also lacked much other useful information. The organisers of the operation therefore used every source they could to collect relevant information, including magazines and tourist leaflets. It was then that Calvão received good news from Lisbon. A Portuguese marine named Alfaiate, who had deserted and fled to Guinea-Conakry, had 'repented' and returned. The marine knew Conakry well, and it was thanks to information provided by him that it was possible for Calvão to locate the targets on a map of the city.[4] The initial plan included a high number of targets that had to be reduced, but since the operation was now to be carried out at a weekend – when the public services were closed and many of the military and paramilitary forces would be at home – there was no longer the need for so many targets. The number of targets thus dropped from 52 to 25, with each being allocated an attack team, varying in personnel and type of weaponry.[5] The military map of the city that is reproduced in this book reveals many of the initial targets that were selected, which shows the ambition of Calvão's original plan. This map served as a basis, together with nautical charts collected from merchant ships sailing from the port of Conakry, for one of the officers on the flagship, LFG *Orion*, to produce maps that were distributed to those who were to lead the various attack groups. Many of the targets on this map were secondary ones (with the exception of the airport) and would eventually be discounted during the operation.

This map was subsequently handed over by the LDG (large landing craft) *Bombarda*'s commander, Lieutenant Captain Aguiar de Jesus, to one of his officers, 2nd Lieutenant RN Ferreira Marques, who kept it for 50 years.[6]

The city of Conakry, about which the Portuguese knew very little at the time. (Albert Grandolini Collection)

Soviet weapons

The operation was prepared with great care to disguise the Portuguese involvement, which led to the purchase of arms in Bulgaria similar to those used by the Guinean forces and the making of uniforms akin to those they wore.[7]

The cover-up even reached the point where all white Portuguese military personnel involved in the operation were forced to paint their faces black to give the impression they were African. Their weapons – Kalashnikov assault rifles, rocket launchers, mortars and associated ammunition – were purchased through Norte Importadora, Lda, a company run by Portuguese businessman José

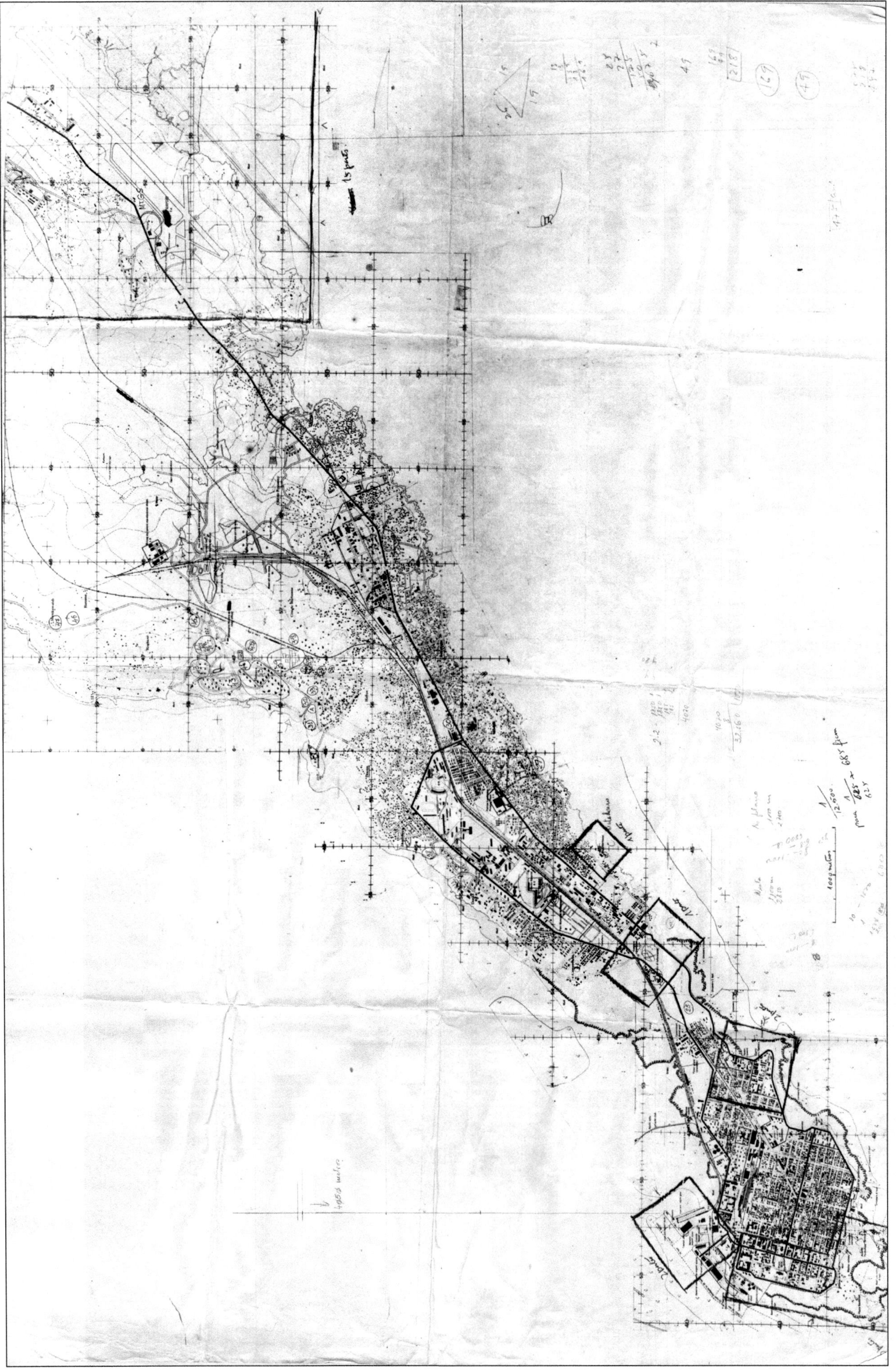

Map of the city of Conakry, with some of the targets for the operation marked. (Ferreira Marques Collection)

Joaquim Zoio, who knew the French arms dealer Georges Starckmann. Zoio, who had links with the PIDE, received Starckmann in his office in Lisbon and told him he needed to buy Russian armament to equip a 300-man combat group for a "very special and secret operation".[8] The Frenchman then made the necessary contacts with one of his usual suppliers: Kintex in Bulgaria. Starckmann pretended that the destination of the weapons was Nigeria, and after payment was made in dollars, Kintex delivered the war materiel to Sofia airport.[9] The weapons were then loaded into a transport aircraft rented from a Belgian company, with Lagos in Nigeria as their final destination, but stopping en route in Lisbon. Starckmann later recalled: "The material was unloaded in Lisbon by soldiers warned of the arrival of the plane, then quickly transported by truck to a military camp near Lisbon, all under military control of [the] PIDE."[10]

The African commandos dressed in uniforms similar to those of the Guinean forces. (Luis Costa Correia Collection)

Thierno Diallo when he served in the French colonial army in Algeria. Diallo received a vote of confidence from Calvão for Operation Mar Verde, and was selected to replace Sékou Touré if the coup was successful. (Albert Grandolini Collection)

Although Kintex was a Bulgarian firm, the weapons were Soviet-made, which may have meant the KGB (*Komitet Gosudarstvennoi Bezopasnosti*) was aware of the deal; however, it is doubtful whether it knew the final destination of the weapons or whether it eventually warned the Guinean regime of the shipment. Nevertheless, the serial numbers of the weapons were all erased by the Portuguese to prevent their origin from being identified.

Meanwhile, talks were held to form a new government for the Republic of Guinea (which had several versions), with David Soumah appointed as chief of state.[11] However, the notorious divisions within the FLNG led Spínola and Calvão to go to Paris in September 1970 to reconcile David Soumah and Thierno Diallo, who had cut off relations; otherwise, the Portuguese government would suspend its support. The meeting was carefully staged to bring together Soumah and Diallo, who eventually agreed to carry out the operation.[12] However, after that meeting, Calvão decided that Soumah could not be trusted, and switched support to the FLNG faction represented by Thierno Diallo and Hassan Assad.[13]

After several months of military training by Portuguese instructors, the Guinean personnel were joined by a detachment of African special marines and a company of the African Commando Battalion. The marines were commanded by Cunha e Silva, while the African Commando company was under the orders of João Bacar Djaló.[14]

In both cases, they were black troops well prepared for special operations and had the advantage that they could be confused for Guinean forces, thus concealing Portuguese involvement. However, these forces had no joint training with the Guineans before the operation. When they arrived in Soga, both the commandos and the marines were kept on the boats, without any contact with the forces that were on the island, in order to guarantee the secrecy of the operation. For their part, the recruited Guineans had little military experience, were not always disciplined and obviously did not have the same fighting skills as the African

African commandos during a ceremony. This special troop was recruited from the local population, and was chosen to go to Conakry because it had the advantage of being black and highly efficient in combat. (Alvaro B. Geraldo Collection)

special forces. Another problem that emerged during the course of the operation was the issue of communications, which did not always function between the various groups involved.

In the meantime, the order of operations was outlined by Calvão, with several objectives in mind: 1) to destroy the central HQ of the PAIGC in Conakry; 2) to release the Portuguese prisoners held hostage by the guerrillas; 3) to destroy the PAIGC and Republic of Guinea vessels in the port of Conakry; 4) to destroy the MiG fighters of the Guinean Air Force, which were based at the airport in the capital; 5) to provide for the landing of FNLG elements.[15] The most ambitious goal of the operation was to support the *coup d'état* and create conditions for the FNLG dissidents to take power in the capital. If that was achieved, the situation would become extremely difficult for the PAIGC.

The first doubts

However, the forces involved only learned the details of the operation a few days before their departure.[16] Thierno Diallo himself was only informed of Calvão's plans shortly before, when he arrived in Guinea-Bissau.[17] Arriving from Lisbon on a commercial flight, Diallo was received by Spínola at Bissalanca airport and then flown by helicopter to the island of Soga, together with the general, with no time to familiarise himself with the personnel he would command. On the morning of 20 November, Spínola paid a visit to LDG *Montante*, which was in Soga, to give a motivational speech to the African commandos because the force led by Major Leal de Almeida had refused to participate in the forthcoming mission.[18]

The officer had expressed great reservations about his participation in an operation against a sovereign state with which Portugal was not at war. It was Spínola who finally convinced him, just two days before the scheduled date for the mission, at a meeting in Bissau.[19] At the preparatory meeting for the operation, Costa Correia, the captain of one of the ships involved, LDG *Montante*, also said that he did not look favourably on the execution of an operation so risky that it could further isolate Portugal internationally, but that he would nevertheless carry out the mission with all the tasks assigned to him.[20]

It was while on Soga, on 20 November, that Diallo was informed of the operational plan and asked that various changes be made regarding the objectives to be achieved. Spínola refused,

General Spínola speaks to the African commandos before departure. (Luis Costa Correia Collection)

Another view of Spínola's speech to the African commandos. To the left of the general, behind the commander with a megaphone, is Alpoim Calvão. (José Manuel Saraiva Collection)

arguing that such a course could postpone the departure of the troops, scheduled for the end of that day. Diallo was told that the timing of the operation had been chosen according to the most favourable conditions for disembarkation, for which reason the plan could not be changed. Spínola sought to eliminate the disagreement with a provocation: "Are you afraid, my commander, to participate in the liberation of your country?" Diallo did not vacillate, but declined any responsibility for the implementation of the plan along the approved lines.

The Portuguese Navy had mobilised most of its resources in Guinea for the operation, specifically four large surveillance boats (LFGs) and two large landing craft (LDGs), which were disguised for the mission to avoid any risk of identification. Marcello Caetano's orders were clear on this matter: the Portuguese forces could not leave any trace in Conakry. The boats and captains involved were as follows:

LFG *Orion* (Lieutenant Captain Faria dos Santos)
LFG *Cassiopeia* (Lieutenant Captain Lago Domingues)
LFG *Dragon* (1st Lieutenant Duque Martinho)
LFG *Hidra* (1st Lieutenant Fialho Góis)
LDG *Bombarda* (Lieutenant Captain Aguiar de Jesus)
LDG *Montante* (1st Lieutenant Costa Correia)

Alpoim Calvão was on board LFG *Orion*, which was the flagship of the flotilla, and with him were the marines that would attack the PAIGC and Guinea-Conakry vessels. LFGs *Dragão* and *Cassiopeia* also had African marines who would attack the PAIGC headquarters, Sékou Touré's summer residence, a militia camp and the prison where the Portuguese were being held. On LFG *Hidra* was a team of African commandos with some Guinean elements, whose mission was to destroy the MiG fighters at the capital's airport. LDG *Bombarda* had another group of African commandos, together with FLNG fighters and guides, who were expected to attack the Presidential Palace, the Interior Ministry, the police headquarters, the railways, the post office and the national radio, as well as dealing with the Cuban contingent. These attack groups were to isolate the coastal part of the city from the rest, since Conakry had an isthmus linking the two parts of the capital. If this isthmus was occupied, the coastal area would be cut off, thus preventing any military reinforcement coming from the north.

Finally, LDG *Montante* followed with another FLNG combat group, along with the African commandos and Guinean leaders such as Thierno Diallo, the Guinean military commander, Hassan Assad, who was to be appointed as future Prime Minister, and Siradiou Diallo, a journalist who could become Information Minister. The objectives of this group were the city's power station, the Republican Guard barracks and the Samory Military

LFG *Cassiopeia*, one of the ships that took part in the operation, sailing on the River Cacheu. (BCM-AH)

On board LDG *Montante*, officers of the Portuguese Navy with the leaders of the FLNG who would attack the Samory Military Camp. The Portuguese officer in the centre is Luís Costa Correia, the ship's captain. (Luís Costa Correia Collection)

Camp.[21] If the coup was successful, Diallo and Assad were intended to occupy the most important positions in the state hierarchy, bypassing David Soumah, who was left behind in Lisbon and took no part in the operation.[22]

Before the task force left Soga on 20 November, maritime reconnaissance missions had already been carried out by P2V-5 Neptunes of the Portuguese Air Force. These planes took off from the island of Sal to detect warships or any concentrations of fishing boats that could reveal the location of the naval force on its way to Conakry.[23]

With nothing special to report, the boats left the island on the night of the 20th for a voyage that would last just over 24 hours. The six boats contained the various assault groups in their green uniforms and distinct yellow hats.[24]

The 120-mile trip was covered during the day by a P2V-5 Neptune to help the flotilla avoid being discovered by unfriendly boats.[25] On the night of 21 November, they finally sighted the lights of Conakry and, keeping a prudent distance, awaited the favourable tide to start the attack in the early hours of the morning. The night was clear, and the waning moon would not rise until 0200 hours. Four ships (LFG *Orion*, LFG *Cassiopeia*, LFG *Dragão and* LDG *Montante*) positioned themselves north of the capital, from where the main attack groups in rubber boats would depart. The remaining two ships (LDG *Bombarda* and LFG *Hidra*) positioned themselves further south.

The LDG *Montante* on the island of Soga with an LFG moored to starboard. (Luis Costa Correia Collection)

The first attack was executed from LFG *Orion*, shortly after 0100 hours, by a group of 14 African marines and a Guinean guide (Victor group) under the orders of Rebordão de Brito, against the torpedo boats of the PAIGC and the

A P2V-5 Neptune from the Portuguese Air Force that was used for surveillance of the route the Portuguese were going to take to Conakry. (Conceição e Silva Collection)

One of the primary objectives of Operation Mar Verde was the elimination of MiG-17s of the Guinean air force, allegedly based at the airport of Conakry. The jets in question were provided by the USSR in the mid-1960s and operated by a small squadron. The only existing photograph of any of them shows a MiG-17 without afterburner, illustrated on the cover of this volume. By 1970, they were reinforced by a handful of MiG-17Fs, one of which is illustrated here: like earlier examples, they were painted in dark green on top surfaces and sides, and light admiralty grey (BS381C/697) on undersurfaces. Despite Portuguese concerns, most Guinean MiGs were non-operational, and only one was made flyable in reaction to Operation Mar Verde. Even so, their pilots had very little experience and could have only deployed cannons in combat. It was only in 1973 that the state of the Guinean air force was improved – and then with the help of Cuban advisors. (Artwork by Paulo Alegria)

Bought from West Germany in 1966, the Fiat G.91R-4 was the only jet fighter that the Portuguese had in Guinea. As of 1970, all were operated by No. 121 Squadron 'Tigers', home-based at Bissalanca AB, outside Bissau. They performed interdiction strikes, close air support and flew reconnaissance. Originally, they retained the camouflage pattern applied by the Luftwaffe, but in 1968 all were re-painted as shown here, in light grey overall. This example is shown equipped with drop tanks on the inboard underwing pylons, and US-made AN-M64 100lb bombs. In the event of the success of Operation Mar Verde, they were prepared to strike insurgent bases close to the border of Portuguese Guinea; the type lacked the range to reach targets deeper in Guinea-Conakry. (Artwork by Paulo Alegria)

The Lockheed P2V-5 Neptune was a US-made maritime patrol aircraft, which Portugal acquired second-hand from The Netherlands. In Portuguese service, they retained the livery consisting of bluish grey on top surfaces, and white everywhere else. Detachment 61 of the FAP deployed two from Cape Verde airport starting from 1961, in support of the Cape Verde and Guinea Air Zone (ZACVG). During Operation Mar Verde, one P2V-5 was forward deployed on Sal Island, from where it ran maritime reconnaissance operations, searching for any kind of boats that could detect the approach of the Portuguese naval vessels. The aircraft could be armed with bombs ranging from 50 to 340kg, and also torpedoes, depth charges, and sea mines (all carried internally) or with unguided rockets (installed underwing). (Artwork by Paulo Alegria)

During Spínola's time as commander-in-chief in Guinea, the Africanisation of the conflict reached its peak with the formation of companies of African commandos made up exclusively of local recruits. These troops were commanded at the highest levels by white officers, however, at intermediate levels they had black officers in command, like the one we see here with his red beret and the metallic badge of the Commandos displayed during a military ceremony. The boots are the regulation ones of the Portuguese Army, while gloves and white laces are exclusively ceremonial items. The uniform appears to be Model 2G, introduced during the 1960s. The camouflage is in the "Lizard" pattern, created by the French, although the Portuguese variation had vertical patches (in the original pattern they were horizontal) and darker tones, better adapted to forest environments. The canvas belt appears to be a copy of the American Model 1956. The scarf at the neck and the metal badge on the chest are typical of a wide range of non-official items common at the time. The weapon is a G3 rifle, in 7.62 mm calibre, as used by the Portuguese forces. In the final years of the war, these types of forces played a decisive role in operations carried out not only in their home territory, but also in neighbouring countries, as in the case of Mar Verde in Conakry. (Artwork by Anderson Subtil)

To avoid Portugal being associated with the invasion, the troops deployed for Operation Mar Verde troops all wore a non-standard uniform model made in Portugal. The green uniform worn by this white officer is an example of this, bearing no resemblance to what the Portuguese troops were wearing at the time. The jungle hat also follows the same concept, although his shoes are the jungle boots worn by the paratroopers and other elite Portuguese troops in Africa. The wide leather belt with large metal buckle seems to have been adopted with the same intent as the uniform, although it does not appear to be comfortable at all. The ammunition pouches are the same as those of the Bulgarian Army and certainly came along with the Bulgarian-made copies of 7.62 x 39 mm Kalashnikov assault rifles. It is worth remembering that the Bulgarian variants were a little different from the Soviet original and characterised by great reliability and the quality of their raw materials. The weapons used in the operation were all purchased in Bulgaria. The white officers who took part in the operation painted their faces black so that they would be confused with the Guinean troops. (Artwork by Anderson Subtil)

PAIGC

UNIDADE E LUTA

The light brown uniform shown in this illustration was the model most used by PAIGC members as of 1970, but by no means the only one, as there was a variation in green cloth and East German uniforms with a "raindrop" camouflage pattern were also used. The jungle hat is the same as worn by the Soviet Army and this particular item seems to have been much appreciated by various African guerrilla movements, as it appears amongst the clothing of guerrilla members in various countries and colonies. The rifle is a Soviet AKM with a calibre of 7.62 x 39mm. In 1970, the PAIGC had around 6,000 combatants and, of this number, 4,800 men were engaged in operations within Guinea's territory. The PAIGC combat units were well armed and in some cases had better weapons than the Portuguese troops. Its members were trained in friendly communist countries and locally had complete freedom of movement in neighbouring countries, which gave them a great advantage over the Portuguese forces. During the invasion of Conakry several PAIGC members were killed in the town's port during the attack on the guerrilla boats and at party headquarters. (Artwork by Anderson Subtil)

In Guinea, the Portuguese Navy had four large surveillance launches (LFG), the first of which had arrived there in 1964. The LFG *Cassiopeia* illustrated here was constructed at the Alfeite shipyard in Lisbon, as the fifth out of ten vessels that made up the *Argos*-class. It was a ship adapted to the extensive Guinean river network and it was there that it made its operational life until September 1974, when the Navy decided to sink the ship, off Guinea, as it was considered that its condition did not justify repair. The *Cassiopeia* had a maximum displacement of 210 tonnes and could reach 17 knots. The ship was armed with two Bofors 40/60 mm cannons and two 7.62mm MG42 machine guns. Before Operation Mar Verde, in September 1969 this ship made a night reconnaissance mission to the port of Conakry and returned undetected. A year later, it integrated the Mar Verde Task Group, together with the LFG *Cassiopeia*, *Hidra* and *Orion* and the LDG *Montante* and *Bombarda*, having been involved in the transport and disembarkation of the combat groups engaged in the invasion of Conakry. (Artwork by Paulo Alegria)

Since 1967, the Portuguese had information about the deliveries of Soviet-made Projekt-183 or P-6 motor torpedo boats to Conakry. In reality, the vessels had no torpedo capacity installed; instead, they had turrets with two 25mm 2M3 autocanons installed forward and aft as their only armament. Capable of reaching speeds in excess of 40 knots, the P-6s were crewed by PAIGC members trained in the Soviet Union and could rapidly attack enemy vessels. However, these vessels were stationary in the port of Conakry, probably for fear of the Portuguese Navy or aviation that could easily attack this type of ship. Moreover, the training of the crews was deficient and their ability to operate these vessels was not the best and it is doubtful that they had the capacity to carry out long-distance operations in the waters of the Portuguese colony. Even so, they were seen as a threat by the Portuguese forces and were one of the main targets during the invasion of Conakry, being destroyed in the port. (Artwork by Paulo Alegria)

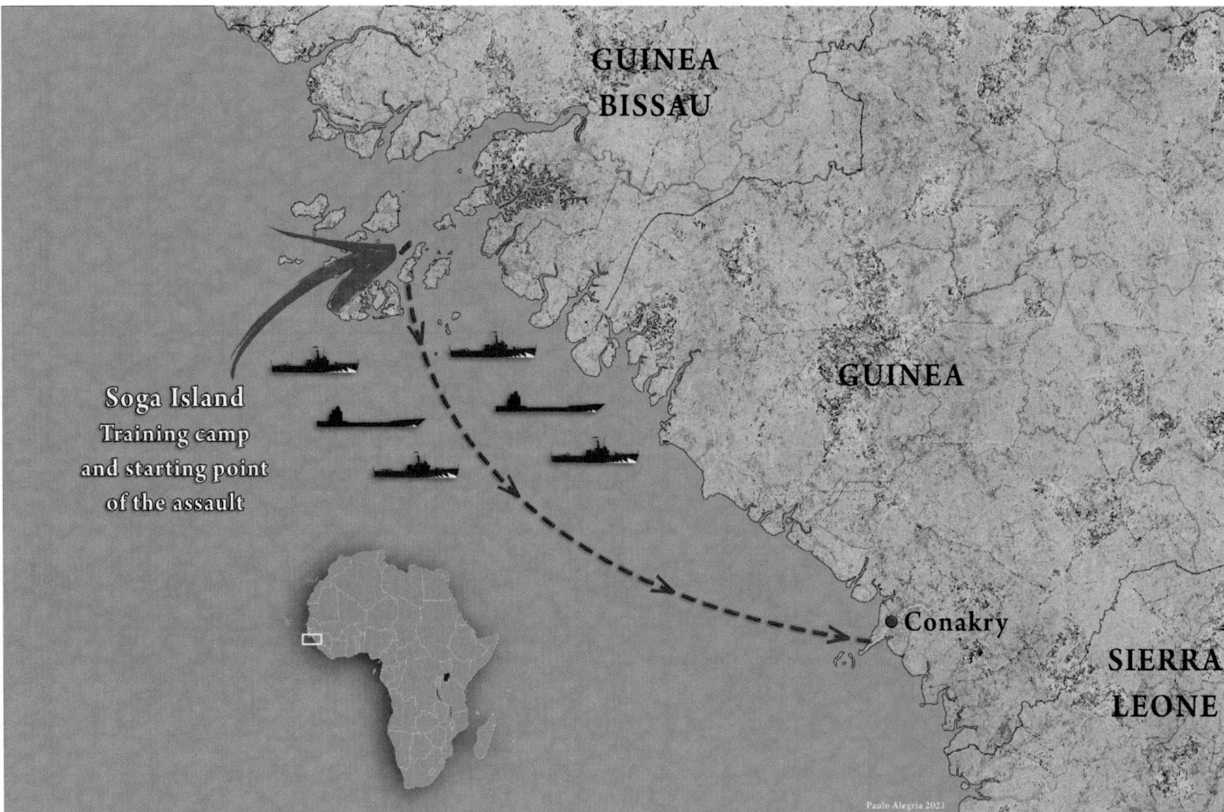

This map shows the approach routes used by the Portuguese forces for Operation Mar Verde. Together with Guinean dissidents, they left the island of Soga on 20 November on a 120-mile journey that would end in Conakry. During the journey the Portuguese boats avoided fishing boats, which could alert the neighbouring country's authorities. For this, they relied on a P2V-5 Neptune, which made several reconnaissance flights to ensure that the Portuguese force would not be detected. The arrival in the neighbouring capital occurred during the night of 21 November, which helped ensure that the ships were not spotted from the city. Once they arrived in Conakry, the boats would wait until dawn to start their attacks. (Map by Paulo Alegria)

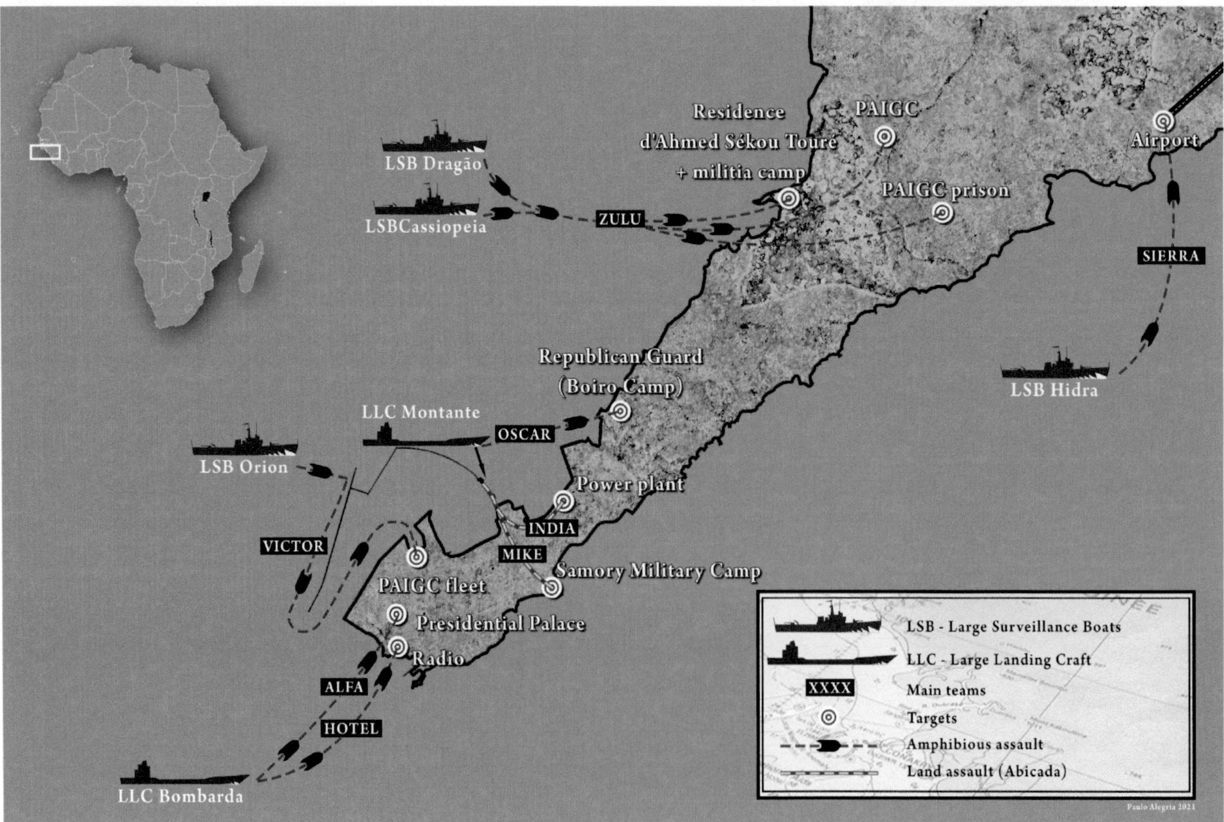

This map shows the deployment of the Portuguese naval vessels around Conakry, during Operation Mar Verde. The four LFGs always kept a distance from the city by landing the attacking forces in rigid inflatable boats. The two LDGs moved closer and the LDG *Montante* was the only vessel to put ashore and land forces directly. The command of the operation was aboard LFG *Orion*, which would launch the first attack against the port of Conakry, where the marines attacked the PAIGC and Guinean Navy boats. After this first attack other groups reached the city to hit the planned targets. This naval configuration would be maintained practically from dawn until the end of the operation. With the uncertainty caused by the absence of the MiGs at the airport, Alpoim Calvão would eventually withdraw to avoid any attack by these fighters. (Map by Paulo Alegria)

The Samory military camp occupied by the attacking forces. (Albert Grandolini Collection)

Guinean Navy that were in the port. The marines embarked in three rubber assault boats and headed for the breakwater that protected the port of Conakry. Arriving there, Rebordão de Brito climbed the breakwater and tried, with the help of binoculars, to locate the enemy boats. He was amazed to see what appeared to be the silhouette of a frigate, which de Brito imagined could only be Soviet. Attacking a frigate with such a small group was a suicide mission, but the marines, without hesitating, went around the breakwater to the south and entered the small inlet of the harbour towards the dock, without being noticed. During the approach, they discovered that what had seemed to be a frigate's silhouette was only that of two superimposed boats that in the distance looked much bigger. The marines eliminated the PAIGC lookout who was on the pier and attacked the ships with grenades, causing great damage. Although caught by surprise, some members of the garrison still managed to put up a fight, but the attacking force eventually prevailed.[26] Suffering only a minor injury, Rebordão's team left the harbour, leaving behind seven burning boats and 15–20 dead PAIGC fighters. Domination of the waters off the city was thus assured; the invading force could not have risked an attack from these boats, either during the operation or when it was withdrawing.

Shortly after this attack, the city was plunged into darkness due to an attack against the power station carried out by a group of 10 African commandos (India group) from LDG *Montante*, led by Furriel Demda Sêca, who eliminated the sentries at the power station and cut the lights.[27] This LDG had already launched the Oscar team at 0135 hours, comprising 40 men who had the objective of attacking the Camp Boiro barracks manned by the Republican Guard. After this first group had been dropped off in boats, LDG *Montante* approached the breakwater around the port from the north and approached the pier, where it landed two more teams: one that went to the power station (India) and the Mike group with 50 men (15 African commandos and 35 FLNG personnel), led by African commander Sisseco and Commander Diallo of the FLNG. The latter team headed for the Samory military camp, headquarters of the Ministry of Defence and the General Staff, where it overcame the sentries and occupied the premises, and then ambushed a military column that approached the camp.[28]

This barracks contained a large quantity of war materiel and was the central point for the Guinean forces to obtain their weapons, but when the column arrived they were surprised by the African commandos. Meanwhile, the Oscar team was attacking the Camp Boiro barracks of the Republican Guard, where they released political prisoners of the regime, although they suffered a fatal casualty, Rodrigues Ferreira, who commanded the group.[29] When the commandos arrived at the gate of the barracks, they

The PAIGC prison after the assault. In the background can be seen the hole opened in the prison wall by the Portuguese forces. (via Albert Grandolini)

Portuguese prisoners in Conakry. (via Albert Grandolini)

realised that some civilians, who had seen the troops, had warned the soldier at the gate, who closed the entrance. One of the African commandos, Marcelino da Mata, jumped through the window of the guardhouse and cut down the sergeant who was there with a sabre, then opened the gate from the inside. However, when the attacking force entered, Rodrigues Ferreira was mortally wounded in the head by a burst of machine-gun fire.[30]

Camp Boiro was the regime's prison, run by a nephew of the dictator, Siaka Touré, who took refuge during the attack in a nearby hotel, the Camayenne.[31] Meanwhile, General Lansana Diané, the regime's Minister of Defence, was captured at the entrance to the barracks and handed over to the FLNG elements who remained at Camp Boiro.[32] This barracks normally housed a large number of military personnel, but as it was the weekend, it was impossible to determine how many would be there. Marcelino da Mata claimed that there was a full regiment inside and that he himself killed 94 soldiers.[33]

Meanwhile, at 0100 hours, the LFGs *Dragon* and *Cassiopeia* that were anchored further north dropped the Zulu team marines, which split into three groups: one, led by Lieutenant Cunha e Silva, went to the prison of the PAIGC, where the Portuguese prisoners being held were to be released. Another group, led by Lieutenant Falcão Lucas, attacked the PAIGC headquarters in search of Amílcar Cabral, and the last section, under Lieutenant Benjamin Lopes de Abreu, attacked a militia camp and the home of Sékou Touré, where it was thought the dictator might be.[34] The attackers' progress through the city was not easy, with the FLNG guides struggling to find some of the targets. Sékou Touré's residence, which was in the Bellevue district, also had

The national radio station, *Voice of the Revolution*. (Albert Grandolini Collection)

Amílcar Cabral's house in Conakry, which was destroyed in the Portuguese attack on 22 November 1970. (via Albert Grandolini)

Destruction of the PAIGC General Secretariat after the Portuguese attack on Conakry. (via Albert Grandolini)

The house of Amílcar Cabral after the Portuguese attack on Conakry. (via Albert Grandolini)

Amílcar Cabral with Aristides Pereira and Pedro Pires in Conakry. None of the main PAIGC leaders were captured during the operation. (Amílcar Cabral Foundation)

a guardhouse. However, the marines commanded by Lopes de Abreu ended up going to the wrong house, that of the bishop of Conakry. With people at the bishop's residence telling the marines where Sékou Touré's house was, they finally arrived at the right location, shot the two guards who were on watch and entered the property. However, they did not find anyone inside; the house had not been used that night. Nevertheless, Lopes de Abreu ordered the house to be destroyed, which was done using rocket launchers and hand grenades. A car belonging to Sékou Touré was also destroyed.

Meanwhile, the group advanced to the Popular Militia Camp, located some 100 metres away, where personnel had reacted to the attack on Sékou Touré's house. Lopes de Abreu's marines caught many soldiers in the barracks, attacking with hand grenades and rocket launchers and causing several deaths and injuries. During the attack, a Volkswagen car was also hit, which was driven by Count Otto von Tiessenhausen, a West German involved in cooperation and aid programmes for the Guineans. Tiessenhausen eventually died from his wounds, although he was later accused of being an accomplice of the Portuguese during the invasion.[35]

A little further east, in the city, Lieutenant Cunha e Silva's group reached the PAIGC prison, a property with a high wall around it. The guards opened fire on the attacking force, causing serious injury to one of the group, but the marines responded with bazooka fire which opened a hole in the prison wall. Entering the building, they released the 26 prisoners they found there.[36]

In Bissau, the Maritime Defence Command and PIDE/DGS followed the progress of the attack throughout the dawn through the messages they received from Calvão, and which Matos Rodrigues then transmitted to Lisbon to the headquarters of the PIDE/DGS:

> Disembarkation of forces Green Sea Operation held one hour Conakry. PAIGC facilities totally destroyed. Amílcar Cabral absent foreigner. Release twenty-six national military prisoners including Sergeant Lobato. Seven boats destroyed. Coup d'état dubious but as yet unknown results will follow. Further details soon to be known. Respectful greetings Matos Rodrigues.[37]

In fact, most of the objectives were successfully achieved, but there were also notable failures, such as the attack on the national radio station, *Voice of the Revolution*, apparently due to the disorientation of the team charged with taking this objective.[38] The radio station was targeted by a group of African commandos from

LDG *Bombarda* (Hotel team), commanded by Ensign Jamanca, who disembarked at the quayside of the port of Boulbinet, relatively close to the objective, but was unable to identify it.[39]

The failure to take the radio station prevented the opposition from broadcasting its proclamation, which had already been written to be read out over the radio.[40] The station would subsequently be used by Sékou Touré to call for resistance to the attack.[41]

Another target for the operation was the headquarters of the PAIGC, in the district of Minière, where Amílcar Cabral had his residence, which was attacked with rocket-launcher fire. The elements guarding the house opened fire on the attacking force of Guinean marines commanded by sub-tenent Falcão Lucas.[42]

The leader of the PAIGC guerrillas was not in Conakry, but his wife, Ana Maria Cabral, only narrowly escaped the attack by the invading forces.[43] Other important party leaders, such as Aristides Pereira, were also not found, although information to the contrary was reported to Bissau:

> Aristides Pereira number two PAIGC was shot down during an attack in which more than 50 persons [were] in charge. Fight continues [in] Conakry. 120 political prisoners were released and armed and attacked Sékou Touré forces causing 500 deaths. Matos Rodrigues.[44]

The fear of the MiGs

Another important objective was Conakry airport, where the MiG-17 fighters of the Guinean Air Force were believed to be, which had to be eliminated in order to ensure aerial control.[45] These fighters of Soviet origin had been supplied to many African countries that had good relations with Moscow, as was the case with the Republic of Guinea. The MiG-17s had three cannons and during daylight hours could obviously attack the Portuguese ships, which did not have much defence against this type of fighter.

The force responsible for the attack on the airport (Sierra team) was dropped from LFG *Hidra* and was led by paratrooper captain Lopes Morais. It consisted mainly of African commandos (33 men), in addition to five FLNG officers, one of whom was a former air controller at the capital's airport, so knew the site well.[46] However, when this group arrived at the airport, already depleted after the desertion of part of the team,[47] they discovered that the hangars were empty. Unfortunately for the attacking force, the MiGs had been sent to Labé, in the north of the country, on 20 November, so were not at the capital's airport.[48] Upon learning of the situation, Calvão sent this group back to the landing site and decided that the operation consequently had to be finished before dawn, given that "one of the factors of success, air dominance, was strongly compromised".[49] Obviously he could not risk a fighter attack against the Portuguese ships compromising the whole mission. In short, two important objectives had not been achieved, and this information was transmitted to Bissau: "Green Sea Operation failed [in] broadcast occupation and there was desertion [of] Lieutenant Januario and 20 African commandos. Fight continues CONAKRY. Matos Rodrigues."[50]

On the Republic of Guinea government side, the Secretary of State for Youth, Alpha Diallo 'Portos',[51] did indeed try to mobilise the MiGs by contacting Captain Sylla Ibrahima, in charge of military aviation, who told him that the fighters were all out of service, but undertook to at least try to get one flying.[52] Alpha Diallo asked him to have the presidential helicopter fly over the capital to make the attackers believe that the president had left the city.[53] In the morning, a MiG fighter jet did manage to take off from Labé to try to intercept the Portuguese forces. Piloted by Lieutenant Hady Canté, the MiG-17 flew over the Guinean capital at low altitude at about 0900 hours, when the Portuguese forces had already re-routed, and detected a boat in Conakry Bay which it believed was an enemy vessel.[54] The pilot opened cannon fire on the ship, which was in fact the Cuban freighter, *Conrado Benitez*, causing injury to a member of the crew.[55] After this episode, the pilot flew over the Portuguese naval force at high altitude, but did nothing to intercept it.[56] However, the appearance of the MiG confirmed that Calvão's decision to withdraw had been the right one, as the Navy's boats did not have an effective anti-aircraft defence and the radius of action of the Portuguese fighter jets did not allow any air cover over the Guinean capital.[57] Calvão later reflected on the situation:

> We had a very big problem, which was our aviation, which did not get there. There was the famous issue of the MiGs who were not in Conakry. I only came to know that the MiG only flew once and badly, after having Lobato on board, at 9:30 in the morning.[58]

Caught asleep

There is no doubt that the operation was a complete surprise to Sékou Touré who, at the time of its launch, was in his palace sleeping.

It seems that the Guinean dictator was already aware of the preparation of a military initiative against Guinea-Conakry, but clearly did not know when this would happen.[59] However, he had received information from neighbouring countries about the movements of the FLNG men, as was highlighted in the previous chapter. In the same vein, Suzanne Cronje wrote in *The Washington*

Conakry airport. (Albert Grandolini Collection)

The presidential palace, where Sékou Touré was on the night of the invasion. (Conakry Presidential Palace)

A T-6 in Guinea with rockets and machine guns. This is a similar aircraft to the one that Sergeant Lobato was flying in 1963 when he was captured. (José Nico Collection)

Post on 24 November 1970, claiming that the invasion could not have taken Sékou Touré by surprise, given the existence of reports of hostile forces in neighbouring countries willing to overthrow the regime.[60] Two months before the invasion, Sékou Touré himself said he knew of a network of mercenaries in Guinea-Bissau and Senegal trained by Colonel Jean Schramme, a Belgian mercenary who had already fought in the former Belgian Congo.[61] The dictator thus had strong suspicions that an invasion could happen at any time, and reported this in his public speeches.[62] In addition, he had given instructions to the armed forces based in Conakry to prepare the defences of the city. In his memoirs, Lieutenant Camara Kaba, a member of Conakry's garrison who would be arrested the following year, reports a meeting at the Ministry of Defence in Campo Samory in mid-1970 between several officers of the General Staff to devise a defence plan for the capital. At that meeting, responsibility for the city's nerve centres was divided among the officers present, who, in the event of an attack, would go to the Samory barracks to take men and weapons to defend their respective sites. Camara Kaba wrote that he was the only one during the meeting who raised doubts about the effectiveness of the plan, saying he wanted to have his men and weapons on hand before the invasion in order to reconnoitre the locations which he was charged with defending. However, his request was refused by Commander Kouroma Soma, Headquarters Battalion Commander, which would prove to be a mistake that would cost the defenders dearly during the invasion.[63]

All these preparations indicate that Sékou Touré did indeed know something, yet when Alpha Diallo called the presidential palace at dawn to find out about the situation, the dictator was completely unaware of what was happening in the capital.[64] Faced with a difficult situation, Diallo decided to join Sékou Touré in the palace to organise the resistance. The dictator was accompanied by several of his ministers and his wife, but no one could decide what to do until Diallo suggested that Touré hide in the house of someone he knew. Consequently, it was decided that the president would leave the palace and go to the home of the mother of the Director General of the Security Services, Guy Guichard, where he would hide until the situation became clearer. Touré thus went to the home of Hadja Néné Gallé Barry.[65] Sékou Touré's escape from the threat of capture allowed him to subsequently appeal to his supporters to resist the invasion using the national radio station, which had not been taken by the attacking forces. Meanwhile, the African commando team of 10 men charged with taking the palace (Alpha team) had been dropped from LDG *Bombarda*, and eventually achieved their objective. The guards at the palace fled when the commandos arrived, but a search of the complex could find no sign of the dictator.[66]

In summary, the Portuguese operation had by this point achieved some notable successes: the release of the Portuguese prisoners held by the PAIGC and the destruction of the ships that were in the port of Conakry, as well as the release of Guinean political prisoners who were in Camp Boiro.[67] However, these successes were of little value to the overall success of the operation. Sékou Touré was still alive and in unknown location, which made the coup impossible. The failure to capture the dictator also showed a poor prioritisation of targets in the order of operations, since in a mission aimed at overthrowing a regime, the capture or elimination of the chief of state should be of the highest priority, above all other considerations.

In terms of casualties, the attacking forces had suffered just three dead, which was far fewer than the Guinean losses. Taking into account the figures given in various reports on the operation, it is easy to arrive at 250 dead among the Guinean forces, plus another 15–20 killed that the PAIGC suffered in the attack on the port.

In a statement to the historian José Freire Antunes, Calvão acknowledged that "the strategic objective had failed" and that the "FLNG was not able to overthrow Sékou Touré's government", but also claimed that "this was not my work, my work was to give them the initial impetus". He added that "in my heart, what I was interested in was bringing in the prisoners, the guys from the FLNG who would hold on".[68] Calvão's confession seems to show that the operation commander's main concern was not the coup d'état, but the release of the Portuguese prisoners of war. Yet this contrasts with the view of Spínola, who saw in Operation Mar Verde a great opportunity to end the PAIGC's influence in Guinea.

Portuguese prisoners on their return to Guinea-Bissau. (Albert Grandolini collection)

Regarding the released Portuguese prisoners, the most famous was the air force pilot Sergeant António Lobato, who had been captured by the PAIGC in 1963 after a bombing mission to the island of Como. During his return to base, Lobato's T-6 suffered a mid-air collision caused by an accompanying aircraft.

The crash resulted in the loss of the second aircraft and the death of its pilot, while Lobato's plane was left without power. Even so, he managed to control the plane and make an emergency landing in a clearing in the Tombali forest, near Catió.[69] However, he was unfortunate to land in a guerrilla-controlled area and was captured and taken to the Republic of Guinea, where he was imprisoned in Kindia. After several years of imprisonment, Lobato organised an escape attempt with two other Portuguese prisoners, but they could not reach the border and were captured after several days on the run. After this escape they were transferred to Conakry, to a PAIGC prison, where numerous other Portuguese prisoners were held. In his memoirs, Lobato describes the experience he had on the night of his release and the welcome he received on LFG *Dragão*:

> Keeping up the pace, we ended up at a beach where we boarded rubber boats towards the high sea. In a few minutes we docked [with] a ship just a few miles from the coast and transhipped.
>
> It is about four thirty in the morning. The LFG *Dragão* crew members do not hide their joy at receiving us on board, but at the same time do not disguise a pious astonishment at our thinness. [Those who are] sailors up to their bones, react to this detail by distributing food and drinks.
>
> Someone who I suppose is the captain, withdraws me from the group and takes me with him to another area of the ship. I hesitate to start eating a delicacy that has been absent from my menu for many years, but even without appetite, I cannot frustrate the affection and hospitality of the sailor.
>
> Despite the delicious taste of rare meat, my first meal in freedom is a fiasco: not only do I have to leave almost half of the snack on the plate, but less than an hour later, I'm here twisting all over with abdominal cramps …

Portuguese boats in the seas off Conakry. (Luis Costa Correia Collection)

Portuguese boats during the operation, with Conakry visible. (Luís Costa Correia Collection)

Sunrise in Conakry. (Luis Costa Correia Collection)

The African commandos returning to Guinea. (Luís Costa Correia Collection)

A parade of Guinean troops in Conakry. (Albert Grandolini Collection)

Someone brings me a glass of whitish water that I take in small sips and that slowly takes effect.

Meanwhile the day is there, in plain sight, full of sunshine.[70]

António Lobato was then taken to LFG *Orion*, where Alpoim Calvão asked him about the MiGs. Lobato said he had heard the MiGs flying above the city a few days beforehand but had not seen them since.[71] At about 0900 hours, the re-embarkation of the troops was complete, Marcelino da Mata's last group of African commandos having boarded LDG *Montante*, which had been ordered to reverse its course and return to the pier in order to collect the officer and his group, who had been delayed because they had tried to bring back some trophies from their mission.[72]

By that time in the morning there had been more than two hours of daylight, leaving the Portuguese naval force exposed to a potential attack by the MiGs. The *Montante* was targeted by some mortar shots fired from the city, but they were very badly aimed. In response, the LDG fired some intimidation shots from its 40mm cannon.[73] After that, the ships left Conakry, arriving back at Soga on the afternoon of 23 November, where the military personnel disembarked to spend the night on the island.[74]

The African commandos remained on the island for about 15 days until they returned to Fá Mandinga.[75] It seems that despite the failure of the mission to instigate a coup, a few dozen FLNG members were still taken to the Guinea-Conakry border and sent to the Koundara area in a desperate attempt to sow rebellion in the north of the country. Several of them were caught and arrested, and others killed by Guinean forces.[76] A similar fate awaited the FLNG members who stayed in Conakry: they were captured and tried by a court, being sentenced to death or to pay heavy penalties.

The 26 Portuguese prisoners freed were transferred to Bissau on 26 November, where they were received by Spínola at the base in Bissalanca. The general praised Sergeant Lobato for his behaviour during his seven years of captivity, during which he always refused to collaborate with the PAIGC; but a deserting soldier who came with the group was punched and kicked.[77] Practically the whole group would be repatriated to Portugal on a cargo plane, with the exception of the defecting soldier and a European civilian living in Guinea.[78] Upon arriving in Lisbon, a major operation was set up to make it appear that the prisoners had escaped alone, without help from Portuguese troops, in order to deny Portugal's involvement in their rescue. In Bissau, the men from the FLNG who had returned were interviewed by Portuguese television and told the story in their own words. They claimed they took part in the attempted coup against Sékou Touré, but then fled to the northern border and entered the Portuguese colony, where they applied for political asylum.

However, in Bissau, Spínola was far from satisfied with the outcome of the operation. In a conversation with Luciano Bastos, commander of the Guinean Maritime Defence, he complained that Calvão had committed unforgivable errors. Spínola even said that Calvão was a complete disappointment and that he would have to give negative references about him to Lisbon.[79] Despite saying this, he ended up praising Calvão for his behaviour during *Mar Verde*.[80]

A Fiat G.91 R4 armed with bombs in Bissalanca. (José Nico Collection)

In his report on the operation, Calvão acknowledged that the objectives on the ground, although in dispute, could have been dominated if he had the time to do so, that is, if he had not been forced to withdraw because they had not ensured air dominance.[81] This was actually the main factor that weighed on the decision to withdraw and prevented the operation from continuing throughout the day. It is an accepted fact that the reaction of the Guinean forces was weak, and that the attackers could have dominated the capital if they had had more time. Jean-Paul Alata, who was a supporter of the Sékou Touré regime, described the situation as he saw it:

> In reality, the mercenaries landed were the undisputed masters of the city from three o'clock in the morning and their final disembarrassment gave rise to perplexing speculation. The apathy of the population was total. The inhabitants dealt with their affairs without haste. They even heard the sound of marimbas, here and there.[82]

This indolence also extended to the Guinean armed forces, which were poorly prepared, with few resources and completely disorganised, as reported by Lieutenant Camara Kaba:

> Unarmed, functionalised, politicised, ragged, barefoot, working on plantations and rice paddies, poorly fed and cared for, the Guinean soldier inspired pity. He had become the target of his people's laughter with which he was silently angry and for a good reason.
>
> This was the state of the Guinean Army in 1970. An unfortunate state, wasn't it? And that was not all. To neutralise him even more, Sékou will set up his Militia against him, well trained by Cubans.[83]

The wounded Thierno Diallo with Hassan Assad on their return from Conakry. (Luis Costa Correia Collection)

In conclusion, Kaba said that "the aggression has found a demoralised, hungry and sick army".[84] In the same vein was the testimony of Al Hassan Diop, who was at the head of the capital's defence forces and was surprised when he sent for weapons from the city's main military camp:

> Sékou has appointed me Chief of Staff of the Defence Armed Forces of the city of Conakry … From that moment on, I was able to realise a number of things … When I sent the teams in search of weapons and ammunition, what was my surprise when someone came to tell me: 'Ah! The key to the ammunition from the Alpha Yaya camp is in the hands of President Sékou'.[85]

A similar impression was shared by the French General Secretariat for National Defence, which in April 1970 had considered the Guinean armed forces to have "a low operational value" and found that they occupied much of their time in "obscure tasks of general interest or propaganda". They were thus "far from their normal military activities" and could not "effectively ensure the training of their personnel" or keep their equipment in working order.[86]

But the Portuguese attack was not only programmed for the capital. In Bissalanca, the Portuguese Air Force was prepared to attack the PAIGC bases on the northern border of the Republic of Guinea. These guerrilla bases had previously been surveyed in photographic reconnaissance missions (RFOT) carried out by the Fiat G.91, a fighter that the Portuguese used in Guinea.[87] When the regime was ousted, these bases were to have been attacked by Portuguese aviation, taking the PAIGC by surprise. The mission was to be carried out by the Fiat G.91, which had the capacity to reach the bases on the border.[88]

Less optimistic in his analysis of the situation was Thierno Diallo in his subsequent report. Wounded during the assault on the Samory military camp, Diallo acknowledged there had been some successes during the operation, such as the release of the Guinean political prisoners in Camayenne (Camp Boiro), and even showed willingness to participate in a new invasion. However, he considered that it would take between 1,000 and 2,000 men to "take and guard the designated strategic points", which was far more than the number used in Operation Green Sea (around 200 men, according to the Guinean commander).[89] The lack of coordination between the various attack groups "at the level of a central command capable of informing and supporting each one of them according to needs" and the failure to take the radio station in Conakry were other negative points pointed out by Diallo. The Guinean commander felt that priority should have been given to the capture of Sékou Touré and his ministers, "because it was seen that the military camps were only of secondary importance". Consequently, Diallo felt, any future operation would have to eliminate the main figures in the government so as not to run the risk of failing again.[90]

The information gap

For Calvão, the major flaw in the operation was the lack of information, which was not able to provide an updated scenario of what was happening in Conakry. In this regard he wrote the following:

> Although as much information as possible was sought it was found that not all of [it was] accurate. There is therefore an urgent need for an organisation reporting directly to the President of the Council and headed by an Under-Secretary of State to deal with all information problems (in the sense of intelligence). This organisation would also be responsible for planning operations of this kind and for carrying them out, and would pool the necessary resources. The current state of operation of our intelligence services is overwhelming in the absence of a national intelligence strategy. We have even gone so far as to have counterintelligence organisations working on intelligence and having to satisfy three or four different bosses.[91]

The lack of information was mainly attributed to Matos Rodrigues, head of the PIDE/DGS delegation in Bissau, who had closely followed all the preparations with Calvão. He himself would admit this in an interview to the *Expresso* newspaper in 1994:

"I was to blame for the failures .... There was a great difficulty in the information work. The troops never had a real intelligence service. And in the DGS we had no organisation."[92]

In the interview, Matos Rodrigues complained about the lack of informants in Conakry, which prevented him from having up-to-date information. After Mar Verde, Spínola wasted no time in attempting to replace him with Fragoso Allas.

Another problem was that the FLNG did not have much support in Conakry, so the local population turned out to be indifferent to the attempted coup. Jean-Paul Alata reported that "the population did not rise up, as was later intended, to expel the invaders to the sea, but, recognising them as foreigners, denied them all cooperation".[93] Calvão also recognised that "if the men of the FLNG were better coordinated with the opposition, if it existed on land, as they guaranteed, that would be for them [as easy as spreading] bread with butter".[94]

However, in Calvão's view, any change of regime would not have been a lasting one. The expectation was that a new government would last just three to four months, long enough to combat and neutralise the PAIGC, since after that there was a very high risk of direct intervention in the country led by the OAU (Organisation of African Unity).[95]

It is interesting to note that after finishing his commission in Guinea and returning to Portugal, Calvão would be involved in the creation of a secret network of informants in Guinea-Conakry and neighbouring countries, with the support of the Chief of Staff of the Armed Forces (CEMGFA), General Venâncio Deslandes, and the Minister of Defence himself, Viana Rebelo. This 'Marine Dragon' plan would be presented in August 1972 and approved two months later, with the creation of a network of informants, financed by the Portuguese state, in African countries such as the Ivory Coast, Senegal and Ethiopia – in addition to France and Switzerland in Europe – which would collect information of interest to Portugal.[96] This network not only collected information concerning the Republic of Guinea, but also had a special interest in Sékou Touré's state and even financed an opposition newspaper, *La Guinée Libre*, run by Captain Abou Soumah, who had been released from Camp Boiro during the Portuguese attack. Although it was a network focused on intelligence gathering, plans to carry out sabotage and guerrilla operations in Sierra Leone and Guinea-Conakry came to light, but were rejected due to their international implications.[97]

MiGs over Bissau

As had been anticipated, the attack on Conakry was severely criticised by the international community. Consequently, the Portuguese regime, although it denied any involvement, realised that it could never repeat such an operation in Africa because of the risk of a limited conflict becoming more expansive. Rui Patrício, who was Minister for Foreign Affairs at the time, reported that he was taken by surprise by accusations during a visit to Brussels, having to deny that Portugal was involved in the operation.[98] He also revealed that although publicly there was an attitude of condemnation of the military operation, in private the attitude was somewhat different:

> [I]t is interesting to note that in private meetings with ministers or other representatives from various countries, who naturally made different statements in public, they commented to me that it would have been a good idea to overthrow the Sékou Touré government and that they only criticised us for failing in this respect.[99]

However, the condemnation was widespread in international organisations, and African countries such as Nigeria, Algeria, Libya and Sudan even offered military aid to the Guinean regime, which fortunately for the Portuguese never materialised.[100] In Bissau, Spínola was concerned, and on 26 November he wrote a letter to Minister of Defence Viana Rebelo stating that he feared an air strike in retaliation, given that Nigeria had placed "at the disposal of the Republic of Guinea fighters and bombers, ready to take off from Lagos for Conakry, and that they were waiting for authorisation to [fly over] the intermediate countries. The arrival in Conakry of the Commander of the Algerian Air Force has also been signalled."[101] This fear of an air attack led Spínola, on 28 November, to ask Lisbon for a reinforcement of air assets, namely bombers with the capacity for night flight and sufficient radius to reach Conakry and other bases in the Republic of Guinea.[102] These fears seemed to be realised on 13 February 1971, when two MiG-17 fighters – supposedly from the Republic of Guinea – flew over Bissau at low altitude, apparently on a photographic reconnaissance mission to the port and base of Bissalanca.[103] The information was received at the Ministry of Overseas Territories and then transmitted to the Ministries of Foreign Affairs and National Defence, where Viana Rebelo tried to find out from American authorities if it would be possible to provide defensive means to Portugal capable of countering the MiGs. However, he received a negative reply because of the arms embargo that the US had imposed on all parties in the conflict in Africa.[104] The Ministry of Defence was still considering sending back to Guinea a detachment of F-86 Sabre fighters, which had been in the colony at the beginning of the war but were withdrawn due to American pressure.[105] However, these proposals were abandoned so as not to lead to any confrontation with the Americans.

Sentencing at the UN

Following the invasion, Sékou Touré requested military assistance from the UN, but the Security Council decided only to send a commission of enquiry to Conakry to find out what had happened. Nevertheless, it condemned the invasion without specifying the nationality of the attacking forces.[106] Through its UN representative, Portugal denied any involvement, but the commission – comprising representatives from Colombia, Finland, Poland, Zambia and Nepal – arrived in Guinea on the morning of 25 November.[107] On the next day, *The New York Times,* through a correspondent from Dakar, reported that Sékou Touré was continuing to call for military support from friendly countries outside Africa to combat a new series of "enemy incursions".[108] The newspaper also reported that Colonel Schramme, a former Belgian mercenary in the Congo whom Touré had accused of being involved in the invasion, was actually raising chickens on a farm in Portugal, and that he had nothing to do with events in Conakry.[109] The UN commission began its work on 26 November, interviewing Ismael Touré, Finance Minister and Sékou Touré's younger brother, who attributed responsibility for the invasion to Portugal on the basis of the testimonies of Portuguese African commandos who had deserted.[110] In essence, the members of the commission listened to witnesses that the regime allowed to speak to them, and delivered its final report to the UN Security Council on 3 December. The document was examined and voted on at a meeting on 8 December, resulting in the condemnation of Portugal, with 11 votes in favour and four abstentions – from France, Great Britain, Spain and the USA. Although it was a strongly worded condemnation with a claim for damages, it did not impose economic sanctions on Portugal, which would probably have led to London or Washington using their veto. Nor did it satisfy Sékou Touré's request to send airborne troops to Guinea, although the resolution clearly left a warning for the Portuguese not to repeat such a feat.[111] Thus, there is no doubt that the Guinean regime benefited from Portugal's condemnation,

Soviet Navy sailors in Conakry. (Albert Grandolini Collection)

A Soviet warship in the port of Conakry. (Albert Grandolini Collection)

New vessels supplied to the PAIGC after 1970. (Fedotikov Gveneja Collection)

Two new vessels supplied to the PAIGC after 1970. (Fedotikov Gveneja Collection)

In September 1971, the Soviets even decided to maintain a permanent naval presence in Conakry in order to discourage any further Portuguese incursion. Consequently, the port of the Guinean capital gained importance in the Soviet naval deployments on the West African coast.[113] In addition to ships, the Guinean regime also authorised the presence of TU-95 Bear D marine reconnaissance aircraft at the capital's airport in 1973. These long-range aircraft could cover a large part of the South Atlantic by making reconnaissance flights from the waters of Brazil to those of South Africa, then returning to Conakry.[114] The facilities for Soviet aircraft in Conakry would, however, be cancelled in 1977, and the naval presence reduced the following year, when Sékou Touré lost some of his interest in Soviet aid.[115]

Moscow has also not forgotten to provide new naval means to Sékou Touré and the PAIGC, with the boats that had been destroyed by the Portuguese during the invasion being restored. In 1973, the Portuguese reported four P-6 class torpedo boats in the service of the Guinean Navy. However, the Portuguese information was incorrect, as the vessels supplied were actually Project 199 boats, very similar to the P-6 and Komar boats that had been destroyed.[116]

mainly because of the solidarity it received from other African countries and Communist states, such as the Soviet Union, which regained influence with Sékou Touré by offering full support to the complaint against Portugal. Relations with Moscow had been affected in 1969 when the dictator discovered contacts between the Soviet embassy in Conakry and conspirators involved in an attempt to overthrow his regime, but support for condemning the invasion meant such 'misunderstandings' were forgotten. In addition, as stated above, Soviet support also extended to naval cooperation, with the presence of military ships in the territorial waters of the Republic of Guinea.[112] Soviet naval visits had begun in 1969, even before the invasion, but they intensified after the Portuguese attack and Moscow's ships became more visible in the region's waters.

The Portuguese estimated that the Guinean Navy had only few personnel, not exceeding 250 men, all recruited from the army. As for the PAIGC, it was believed to have had a staff of 127 men in the navy, with three P-6 torpedo boats (as stated above, this information was wrong as they were in fact Project 199 vessels), in addition to between three and seven landing craft with a transport capacity of between 20 and 30 tons. The torpedo boats could be used as escorts for other PAIGC units, or to transport guerrillas and war materiel between the ports of Conakry, Boké and Kandiafara.[117]

Besides Moscow, Havana also strengthened its influence with the Guinean leader by sending a group of Cuban Air Force technicians and pilots in 1973 to operate the Guinean MiGs, which were practically inoperative.[118] This deployment followed a

Fidel Castro's visit to Conakry in May 1972. (Albert Grandolini Collection)

Several ministers of Sékou Touré's government were hanged from a Conakry bridge, having been convicted of plotting with those behind the attempted coup. (Albert Grandolini Collection)

visit by Fidel Castro to Conakry in May 1972 which strengthened relations between the two countries.

The Cuban advisers also supported the PAIGC, which after the invasion received greater support in its struggle against the Portuguese forces. It was also praise by Sékou Touré himself for the role it had played in defending the capital.[119] For its part, the regime took advantage of the situation to carry out a major purge, arresting hundreds of Guineans accused of participating in

Januário Lopes and other deserters after turning themselves in to the Guinean authorities. (via Albert Grandolini)

the conspiracy, even those who had tried to organise resistance during the attack. On 8 January 1971, the National Assembly was constituted in the Supreme Revolutionary Court, meeting at the People's Palace in Conakry from 18–23 January. Following these popular trials, some 15 ministers were arrested and some even executed, as was the case with Barry Ibrahima, the Minister for Financial Control, who was hanged from a bridge in Conakry.[120]

In addition to ministers, the repression also extended to diplomats, governors, military officers, civil servants, businessmen and foreign nationals.[121] Even the Bishop of Conakry, Raymond-Marie Tschidimbo, was arrested and tried, which led Pope Paul VI to write a letter to Sékou Touré concerned that this cleric might be sentenced to death. In his reply, Touré said that "more than 200 innocent people were victims of the Portuguese aggression in Conakry last November" and that the victims decided "to severely condemn the aggressors and their accomplices", Tschidimbo being among that group. The bishop would be sentenced to forced labour in prison and was only released in 1979.[122]

According to French sources, 91 death sentences were handed down in January 1971, although official sources speak of a lower number of 62.[123] In Sékou Touré's mind, his regime was the target of a permanent imperialist plot with internal complicity, and it was therefore necessary to eliminate those collaborating with the imperialists.[124] As for the LFG *Hidra* African commandos who had deserted on their way to the airport during the attempted coup, they eventually denounced the Portuguese participation but were all executed by Sékou Touré's regime.[125]

The majority of the accused had Guinean nationality, but there were also two German citizens in their number. One of them was Herman Seibold, who ran a vocational training centre in Kankan. On the night of the invasion he was in Kankan, but when he came to the capital in mid-December he was arrested and accused of participating in the conspiracy against Sékou Touré. Seibold would die in prison under mysterious circumstances, but his flat in Kankan was searched and the Guinean authorities claimed to have found a written message dated 24 November, supposedly from Bonn, which revealed West Germany's involvement in the plot.[126] However, this message had actually been falsified as part of the misinformation campaign that East Germany was mounting in Guinea-Conakry to discredit Bonn. The other German prisoner was Adolf Marx, who had been chief of a French brewery for many years. Arrested on 29 December, he eventually confessed everything that Ismael Touré demanded of him as proof of West German involvement in the conspiracy. Fearing for his life, Marx stated that he was supposed to kill Sékou Touré with poisoned beer and that he had been ordered by Count Otto von

Tiessenhausen to carry out economic sabotage in the country, with the German nobleman being involved in the Portuguese invasion. This campaign of deception would eventually lead to the cutting off of diplomatic relations with West Germany and the expulsion of all its diplomatic personnel who were in Conakry.[127]

Meanwhile, some of the weapons used by the attackers were recovered and the dictator was able to determine their origin, which led him to protest to Bulgarian authorities, threatening to denounce the situation to Moscow. The situation became an embarrassment for Kintex, which had to send two representatives to Conakry to buy Sékou Touré's silence.[128]

4
The Impossibility of a Military Solution

The failure of the coup d'état made it impossible to eliminate the advantages that the PAIGC had in Guinea and maintained the status quo. Thereafter, Spínola became convinced of the infeasibility of a military solution, and made his opinion known in Lisbon at a meeting of the Supreme Council for National Defence (CSDN).

In search of a political solution

At the CSDN meeting on 7 May 1971, Spínola gave a long exposé in which he emphasised that the regime must lose any illusion as to the possibility of winning the war, as the problem of Guinea could only be solved at a political level:

> [I]t is not in Guinea that this war is won, but it is in Guinea that we can begin to lose it. And all indications are that this will happen because the enemy does not disarm; and the stronger the ideas around which we can galvanise the people of Guinea, robbing them of subversion, the more violent the reaction of the enemy will be, reflected in the intensification of its guerrilla action; action which our scarce military potential will never be able to cancel out, given the increasing capacity of the enemy and our impossibility of destroying their sanctuaries, situated in the countries bordering on where their armed groups radiate.
>
> We must therefore rule out once and for all the desire to win the war we are facing militarily, which could only be won in the field of arms in the face of an unpredictable turnaround in the present world situation. The problem can only be solved in the political arena, and I would like to believe that such a solution is still viable; but to this end, it is essential as a basic condition to prevent at all costs the worsening of the military situation.[1]

Spínola once again recognised the worsening military situation and considered it essential to invest in the 'Africanisation' of the war, which could have political advantages:

> In my view, we have never had and will never have any choice but to Africanise the problem, thus nullifying the colonial war character with which it presents itself in the eyes of the world and thus creating a conjecture framework capable of promoting a significant evolution of Western public opinion and a reversal of the attitude of moderate African countries, with particular reference to Senegal. And in this sense, the policy under way in Guinea has been oriented towards a piecemeal solution at local level.[2]

In his presentation, it was easy to see from the maps presented that the guerrillas were active practically all over the country, being established in close to 80 percent of Guinea. The assertion that a military solution was unfeasible provoked the disagreement of the Defence and Overseas ministers, who proposed that before a political solution was found a military victory should be achieved. Minister of Defence Viana Rebelo said: "As for the claim that a subversive war cannot have a military solution: I do not share the absolute rigidity of such a claim, while admitting that in a conflict of this nature victory by arms alone is difficult to achieve."[3]

On the same issue, Minister for Overseas Territories Silva Cunha stated:

> The possibility of finding a political solution to a conflict of this nature depends on first obtaining a victory in the field of arms, for this will only be viable if it first demonstrates to the people that force is on our side. In [my] view there is no clear separation between a military and political solution to a subversive war.[4]

These remarks led Spínola to reaffirm that the solution to a subversive war went far beyond the possibilities of a military victory, as could be seen in the case of Vietnam. Consequently, he said, the military effort in Guinea should serve only to gain time while no political solution could be found to the war. But to gain time, Spínola needed the minimum military means, means which were not yet secured in Guinea and which had already been requested in 1968. Viana Rebelo recognised the problem of the shortcomings that the armed forces as a whole felt but said that the problem of Guinea could not be separated from the other theatres of operations.

Another minister who spoke was the Minister of Finance, who expressed concern about the financial effort that the war had demanded, which he said was at a level that could hardly be surpassed, noting that defence accounted for some 41 percent of the budget, and could even reach 45 percent with the allocation of a sum for late payments. Spínola replied that, unfortunately, everything pointed to the belief that defence investment would have to increase because it was necessary to resist and remain until a political solution was found. Prime Minister Caetano said that expenditure on the armed forces had been increasing from year to year, and that the problem was how to make better use of the resources available. The President of the Council also mentioned the work that has been done on the political and diplomatic front to try to convince Portugal's allies of the fairness of the policy pursued. He added that "we must also weigh well the chances of success of special missions whose negative results may have particularly unfavourable repercussions on the achievement of the objectives we are aiming for", in a clear allusion to the Mar Verde

The PAIGC guerrillas, well armed and trained, were increasingly active in Guinea, and the Portuguese authorities recognised their powerlessness to deal with the situation. (INEP)

operation.[5] However, there was scant detail on the possibility of a political solution to the war, something that Spínola had defended in his presentation.

Shortly after this meeting, at the end of June, General Venâncio Deslandes – who was still Chief of Staff of the Armed Forces – visited Guinea to assess the situation. During the days he spent in the colony, Deslandes had the opportunity to talk to various sectors of the armed forces and to ascertain the problems that the Portuguese forces were experiencing in Guinea. Like Spínola, the general recognised the worsening of the military situation resulting from the reaction of the PAIGC to the social policy conducted in Guinea. In Deslandes' opinion, the increase in the guerrillas' military capacity was essentially due to four factors: a) material reinforcement, both in qualitative and quantitative terms; b) personnel reinforcement, with the incorporation of foreign specialists; c) organic changes in combat units, which increased flexibility and control in the execution of actions; and d) tactical changes, reducing the number of commitments, but better selecting targets. He also considered that the current means available to the Portuguese forces "are not sufficient to guarantee the permanence of the successes obtained in the development of the manoeuvre begun about a year ago" and admitted that the guerrillas "may try to impose a solution by force, creating situations of difficult or impossible reversibility not favourable to our authorities".[6]

There was also a fear that the PAIGC may employ "techniques of urban terrorism and sabotage" in the main urban centres of Guinea, which would have serious consequences for the morale of the population, especially the Europeans. Another concern of the military command in Bissau was the possibility of the guerrillas trying to obtain at some point in the theatre of operations "a spectacular military success that could be exploited internationally".[7] The lack of resources was serious, with Spínola not having sufficient troops to ensure the safety of the populations under Portuguese control "and also to constitute, with units in reserve, a manoeuvring force capable of resuming the initiative in the operational field".[8] After his visit, Deslandes drew up a lengthy report on the problems he had detected, which came to the attention of Minister of Defence Viana Rebelo. In the light of the situation, the minister decided to write to Marcello Caetano to express his concern about the position in the colony, where the PAIGC were "making a strong military effort to overcome our resistance". In his opinion, if this were to happen, the negative consequences would be felt in the colony and overseas, increasing the threat to Cape Verde and leaving the white and black populations of Guinea unprotected. In his letter to Caetano, Rebelo also admitted that Guinea's defence "will require new burdens, which have not been within reach of the means allocated to National Defence" and that new means of defence should be allocated to the colony, although he recognised that there was no budget for this.[9] In short, Rebelo confessed to the worrying lack of resources in the face of the worsening situation.

Contacts with Senegal

Meanwhile, in Guinea, Spínola was preparing for a new approach to the war with the mediation of Senegal's President Léopold Senghor, who was concerned about Sékou Touré's growing influence in the region through his support for the PAIGC. The first contacts with Senegal had been established in 1970, even before Operation Mar Verde, when a Portuguese delegation went to Dakar in February of that year and was received by Senegal's foreign and interior ministers. The only proposal that emerged from these talks was to suspend Portuguese military activities in order to give Senegal time to exert pressure on the PAIGC and obtain a ceasefire. However, relations between the two countries deteriorated due to several incidents in the border area, and the Portuguese suspended contacts. In April 1971, the Portuguese Minister of Foreign Affairs, Rui Patrício, met his Senegalese counterpart in Paris to try to resolve the border clashes.[10] The two ministers agreed to set up a joint commission to investigate such incidents. However, the commission would never be set up and Senegal ended up making a complaint to the United Nations against Portugal, which led to a condemnation of the Portuguese state by the Security Council. However, in 1972, Spínola managed to organise a meeting with Léopold Senghor to discuss a possible understanding with the PAIGC. The meeting was authorised by Lisbon in the expectation that Spínola would not make any firm commitments.[11] The meeting took place on 18 May at Cap Skirring in Senegal, near the border with Guinea, where Senghor presented a plan based on three points: a) the establishment of a ceasefire, followed by negotiations with all nationalist movements; b) implementation of a period of internal autonomy in Guinea of at least 10 years; and c) ending this period by granting independence with a view to integration into a future Luso-African community.[12] Spínola received Senghor's plan with enthusiasm, saying it seemed

Caetano arrives at Bissalanca airport during his visit to Guinea in February 1969. At this time he still had no major disagreements with Spínola. (DN)

Caetano and Spínola during their visit to Guinea in 1969. In the following years they would end up in opposite camps regarding the future of the colonies. (Virgílio Teixeira Collection)

However, the plan was poorly received in Lisbon because of the degree of uncertainty it contained and the precedent of opening negotiations with a liberation movement.[14] Marcello Caetano received Spínola on 28 May to tell him that he could not accept a negotiation process in Guinea without doing the same in Portugal's other colonies, refusing any possibility of resolving the Guinea problem separately from the rest of the overseas territories.[15] Caetano went so far as to say that for the overall defence of the overseas territories, he would rather suffer a military defeat in Guinea than make a negotiated agreement with the terrorists.[16] Spínola was shocked by this statement, and the distance between the two did nothing but grow in the following months. Although Spínola insisted that Senghor's proposal should not be rejected, Caetano would not budge from his belief that the Guinea problem could not be separated from the rest of the overseas territories.

For the chief of the government, his greatest concern was Angola and Mozambique, where there was a large white community and where the fate of the Portuguese empire was being played out. It was at this moment that Spínola finally realised that there was no political solution to the conflict, and that conflict was the only option Caetano was defending. In his opinion, "the last opportunity to solve

to him a reasonable proposal to solve the Guinea problem. His enthusiasm was confirmed by Silva Cunha:

> General Spínola returned from the meeting dazzled and convinced that he had the definitive solution to the Guinea problem in hand. In Lisbon, at a meeting attended by the Minister for Overseas Territories, he informed the President of the Council of Senghor's proposal, which he strongly advocated.[13]

the Guinea problem with honour and dignity was lost", but the most serious matter was that the government's lack of political will to solve the conflict "pointed to a tragic outcome, in which the Armed Forces, like [had happened in] India, would once again be the scapegoat for an unviable strategy". The invasion of the Portuguese colonies of Goa, Damão and Diu in 1961 by Indian forces was still very much present in the memory of Spínola, who did not want to see the same thing happen in Guinea. Disappointed by the situation, he began to write a book entitled *Portugal e o Futuro* (*Portugal and the Future*), which would be published by Arcádia

Spínola in Guinea with Costa Gomes in 1973. (Pierre Fargeas Collection)

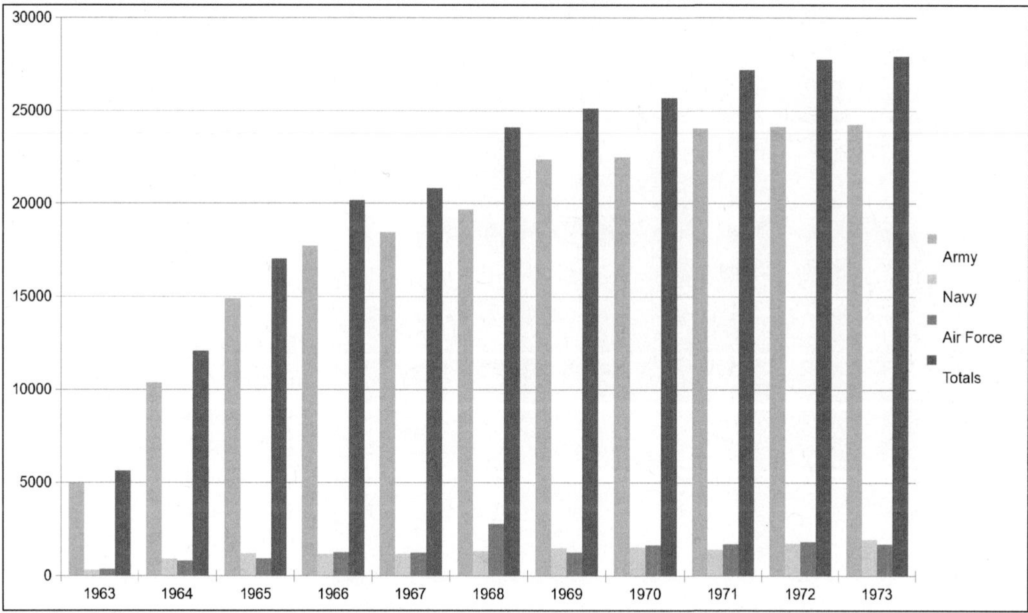

Chart 2 – Evolution of troops in Guinea (1963–1973)

the development of Guinea. However, he foresaw a possible worsening of the military situation as a result of the growing external support that the PAICG was receiving and which might raise the fighting to a new level. He therefore considered it important that "the necessary means exist in the military field to guarantee the balance of forces indispensable to the continuity of that development". These means were not guaranteed, and even the means available to the military command in Bissau were at the limit of their possibilities. Costa Gomes pointed out the shortages of arms and other means to be allocated to troops stationed in Guinea. A table with the PAIGC's military activity was attached to his report, the contents of which are presented here as Table 1.[18]

An analysis of the table shows that the number of actions against Portuguese forces in 1971 and 1972 did not vary greatly from 1970, but the casualties among Portuguese troops reached a new high in 1972, with a record of 919 (as has been stated in Chapter 1, the previous record was 890 in 1970).

Another interesting feature in Costa Gomes' report was the social, cultural and economic promotion of Guineans since the beginning of Spínola's mandate.[19] In his role as governor, Spínola continued to promote works in various locations in Guinea to improve the living conditions of the people, and Costa Gomes seems to have been impressed by what he saw in the colony.

The works already completed between 1969 and 1972 included 83 projects built from scratch that benefited everyone in the settlements. Many of these works were carried out by the military, particularly military engineering projects. The report also pointed out the effort of the Portuguese forces in the southern sector of the colony, in the Cantanhez area, where three military detachments had been installed in a region that was practically a guerrilla sanctuary, where the PAIGC could at any time declare the independence of the so-called 'liberated areas'. There was therefore an urgent need to provide Spínola with the necessary means to guarantee the benefits for the population, although staff shortages were difficult to make up for with personnel from the colony and local recruitment had to be increased.[20] The shortfall in Guinea amounted to some 1,116 men, which Costa Gomes

Publishing in 1974 and which Marcello Caetano would regard as a betrayal of Portuguese government policy.[17]

The visit of Costa Gomes

In January 1973, the new CEMGFA, General Costa Gomes, visited the colony to assess the situation on the ground and noted that the policy of social and economic promotion conducted by Spínola was well accepted by the population, allowing for

Table 1: PAIGC Military Activity		
Actions of the enemy	1971	1972
Actions at the initiative of the enemy	644	726
Reaction actions	441	594
Actions against air transport	2	5
Losses caused to the Portuguese troops	869	919
Casualties caused to the population	711	1,041

Amílcar Cabral with Aristides Pereira in Conakry. The two PAIGC leaders were the main targets of conspirators in 1973. (Amílcar Cabral Foundation)

Naval Elements of the PAIGC captured during an attempt to escape to Bissau after the death of Amílcar Cabral. (Fedotikov Gveneja Collection)

Italian poster of the assassination of Amílcar Cabral advertising a memorial concert on 31 January 1973 at the Teatro delli Arti. (Amílcar Cabral Foundation)

said was not a significant number when considering the overall workforce. However, the problem tended to worsen due to a decrease in the annual contingent, mainly due to the increase in absenteeism, which made it impossible to build up more troops in Africa other than by recruiting Africans.[21] In the case of Guinea, the African force was composed of combat troops and militias and amounted at the end of 1972 to 6,900 men, but the colonial forces had reached their limit and it was not possible to increase their number. It can be seen from the graph reproduced here that the number of troops from Portugal had not stopped increasing since the beginning of the war; in 1971 they had exceeded 27,000 men, but from that moment on there had been a difficulty in increasing the number much further, even though the total did not stop rising until the end of 1973.[22]

The escalation of war

In early 1973, the PAIGC suffered a terrible blow to its leadership when, on the night of 20 January, Amílcar Cabral was assassinated in Conakry by a dissident party faction.[23] The conspiracy is said to have come from navy personnel who, in addition to murdering Cabral, captured Aristides Pereira, the second-in-command of the party, with the intention of taking him to Bissau and handing him over to the Portuguese authorities.

To do so, the conspirators tried to escape in three PAIGC boats that were anchored in Conakry. When Sékou Touré realised the situation, he decided to ask the Soviet Ambassador for help to catch the fugitives. The Soviet Kotlin-class destroyer *Byvaly*, which was in Conakry at the time, was the only naval unit capable of intercepting them. Although the destroyer could supposedly not put to sea without the authorisation of the naval command in Moscow, the ship's commander, Captain Yury Ilinykh, decided to take responsibility for the situation and it seems left shortly after midnight in search of the fugitives, taking on board a platoon of Guinean soldiers. Around 0200 hours, the ship's radar system detected two boats, and some three hours later the Soviet vessel made visual contact with a pair of the PAIGC's torpedo boats, which had dropped anchor because they could not navigate at night.[24] The two boats were captured, but Aristides Pereira was not on board either of them. It turned out that the third boat

Wreckage of a Fiat G.91 shot down by the PAIGC in Guinea with a Strela-2 missile in 1973. (Roel Coutinho Collection)

Gadamael after the PAIGC offensive in June 1973, with evidence of the destruction that the guerrillas caused to the Portuguese outpost. (Delgadinho Rodrigues Collection)

had become lost and returned to shore, and those on board were arrested by the Guinean authorities. They included Aristides Pereira, who was rescued and transported by plane to the capital. The captured sailors were subsequently tried and sentenced to death.[25]

However, the assassination of the PAIGC leader had no effect on the guerrillas' military performance. In fact, contrary to what might have been expected, their situation even improved as they unleashed strong offensives against the border garrisons at Guidage in the north and Guileje and Gadamael in the south. These prolonged attacks in May and June 1973 were made possible by the use of shoulder-fired, surface-to-air Strela-2 missiles supplied by the Soviets, which forced a reduction in the use of Portuguese aviation in both fire and evacuation actions. The first attacks against aircraft took place in the border areas, greatly surprising the Portuguese Air Force, which had not been expecting to face such a sophisticated weapon in Guinea. At the end of March, two Fiat G.91 fighters were shot down in southern Guinea, killing one of the pilots before he had an opportunity to eject.[26]

Shortly after, the missile teams also hit three light aircraft in the north of the territory, killing their crew. With air power thus reduced, the PAIGC forces managed to isolate the border barracks for several weeks with heavy artillery bombardments and ambushes on the access roads, which did not allow any support to reach the garrisons. Although the outpost at Guidage managed to resist, Guileje eventually succumbed to the siege and the Portuguese forces had to leave the barracks, together with the local population.[27] They sought refuge in Gadamael, which became the

The first Popular National Assembly of Guinea-Bissau, in the liberated region of Madina do Boé. Aristides Pereira is shown giving a speech after the PAIGC had declared Guinea to be an independent state. (Amílcar Cabral Foundation)

The parade of the People's Revolutionary Armed Forces after the proclamation of independence at the Madina do Boé assembly. (INEP)

next target of the guerrillas. Within a short time, the guerrillas also attacked this barracks, which was practically destroyed by the PAIGC's intense bombardments. To prevent the abandonment of the garrison, Spínola engaged paratroop forces that were at his disposal, who managed to ease the situation for the defenders.[28]

Nevertheless, the worsening of the situation worried the commander-in-chief, who feared the imminent collapse of the Portuguese forces in the region. To assess the troubling situation, the government sent General Costa Gomes back to Bissau at the beginning of June, and he received from Spínola a list of the reinforcements he considered essential to cope with the new level of fighting.[29] However, Caetano did not have the immediate capacity to satisfy his requests, neither in men nor military equipment. The problem had already been analysed at a meeting of the CSDN convened on 22 May, when the defence chiefs recognised the escalation of the war was due to the guerrillas' use of new weapons such as surface-to-air missiles. In this new situation, the PAIGC clearly enjoyed a greater capacity for manoeuvre due to its defensive capability against Portuguese air power. To counter this escalation, the Portuguese forces urgently needed new armaments. The *Força Aérea Portuguesa* demanded modern Mirage fighters to face the new threat, but the regime found it increasingly difficult to acquire war materiel due to the ongoing arms embargo against Portugal. Defence Minister Viana Rebelo reported that he had sent a company of commandos to Guinea that had originally been heading for Angola, and that two further companies of troops were being prepared to go to Guinea as soon as possible. He also sent aircraft bombs of various types and was preparing to send artillery, but the forces in Guinea required other means that would need to be bought. This required extra funding, which could eventually be obtained from South Africa, with Viana Rebelo having an appointment with his South African counterpart at the end of the month. During the CSDN meeting, Caetano also expressed his concern about the military situation in Mozambique, but recognised that the major problem was in Guinea and that urgent action was needed to tackle the problems, especially in terms of equipment.[30] A week later, the meeting with the South African Minister for Defence took place; consequently, steps began to be taken to guarantee a large loan from Pretoria that would allow an ambitious programme of re-equipment of Portuguese forces to be carried out, but South Africa would not grant the loan until the following year.

On the ground, the situation had deteriorated to the extent there was an increasingly adverse environment for Portuguese troops. The casualties caused by the PAIGC reached a new record of 1,366 in 1973. In the first four months of that year alone, Portuguese forces suffered 321 casualties (33 dead and 288

Caetano and Spínola during their visit to Guinea in 1969. The two men were set on diverging paths after the publication in 1974 of Spínola's *Portugal and the Future*. (DN)

wounded). This number worsened further in the same period of 1974, with 509 casualties (81 dead, 426 wounded and two taken prisoner).[31]

The PAIGC continued to rely on strong international support, in terms of arms, funding and military advisors. Its armament was far superior to that of the Portuguese forces, particularly in artillery, rocket launchers and surface-to-air missiles. In addition, the guerrillas continued to manoeuvre freely in neighbouring countries, moving their forces safely and secretly before launching surprise attacks.[32] One such example had been the attacks in May and June 1973 against the barracks at Guidage, Guileje and Gadamael, which showed that the PAIGC could strike in force in the border areas, having the capacity to isolate and cause great damage to the most exposed garrisons. In turn, the Portuguese forces were exhausted due to inadequate recruitment, were badly trained and lacked the appropriate weaponry to fight the guerrillas. Meanwhile, the PAIGC orchestrated an even bolder initiative with a unilateral declaration of independence for Guinea-Bissau in September 1973. This was carried out in the Madina do Boé region, a deserted area that contained no Portuguese troops, where the PAIGC organised a ceremony with foreign guests, declaring that from that moment Guinea was an independent state. This obviously caused diplomatic problems for Portugal, since the independence was recognised by dozens of countries aligned with the African liberation movements. Portugal was thus seen as an occupying power in Guinea, which only justified the support that the PAIGC had in certain sectors of the international community.

In this situation, the possibility of a military solution favourable to Portuguese interests was pure utopia. Spínola remembered this as the final phase of the Portuguese regime when he published *Portugal and the Future*, where he argued that a military victory in the overseas territories was thereafter unfeasible and that the only solution to the war was a political one.[33] In his opinion, the solution had to be a new political arrangement between Portugal and its colonies, abandoning the previous constitutional model as being too centralised.[34] This solution also implied a certain degree of liberalisation of the regime with the process of self-determination in Africa, so that the African peoples could integrate the future Portuguese community on a voluntary basis through a process of democratic consultation. In addition, Spínola argued that in each of the states of the Portuguese Federal Republic, governors should be democratically elected, as should state parliaments.[35]

Although Caetano was not a democrat, he did advocate progressive autonomy for the colonies which could eventually end in independence, provided the rights of the colonists were guaranteed. For him, what was at stake was not federalism, but guaranteeing the permanence and rights of the white population in a future independent state, a solution that could not be achieved with the liberation movements that, in his opinion, were at the service of foreign interests and wanted to expel whites from Africa. For this reason, he could never accept a negotiation with the PAIGC as Spínola suggested in 1972, as he felt there was the risk of creating a precedent with regard to the other colonies.[36] There was also no guarantee that Amílcar Cabral would be willing to accept Spínola's plan in 1972, since the PAIGC leader has always fought for immediate independence for Guinea and Cape Verde. Although Spínola had the idea of integrating him into the provincial government, it seems clear that Cabral's aim was the construction of an independent Guinea and the withdrawal of Portuguese forces from the colony. Thus, none of the options advocated by Spínola or Caetano were viable as a solution to the war; there was no other path than that of full independence. Even Spínola, who advocated a more progressive colonial policy closer to the people, was only postponing the inevitable. On the other hand, Cabral never showed any interest in negotiating with Spínola. For the leader of the PAIGC, the dialogue would have to be with the central government in Lisbon and not with the provincial governor. This meant that Spínola had been trying to create a solution in Guinea that was doomed from the start, not only because it was on a collision course with the regime's official policy, but also due to it not corresponding to the PAIGC's aspirations. Even the federalist thesis he championed in *Portugal and the Future* was not viable in 1974, as was seen after that year's 25 April revolution in Lisbon that overthrew the country's authoritarian regime and eventually led to a Portuguese democracy.

Bibliography

Archives

National Defence Archive (ADN)
Military Historical Archive (AHM)
Historical Archives of the Presidency of the Republic (AHPR)
Overseas Historical Archives (AHU)
National Library of Portugal (BN)
Central Marine Library – Historical Archive (BCM-AH)
National Archives Institute/Torre do Tombo (ANTT)
Oliveira Salazar Archive (AOS)
PIDE/DGS archive
French National Defence Historical Service (SHDN)

Newspapers

Several newspapers were consulted in the research of this book; these are listed in individual endnotes and not duplicated here.

Books

Airault, Pascal & Bat, Jean-Pierre, *Françafrique, Opérations secrètes et affaires d'Etat* (Paris: Editions Tallandier, 2018)

Alata, Jean-Paul, *Prisão de África* (Lisbon: Edição Livros do Brasil, 1976)

Amado, Leopoldo, *Guerra Colonial & Guerra de Libertação Nacional – 1950-1974 – O caso da Guiné-Bissau* (Portuguese Institute for Development Support, 2011) (PhD thesis defended in 2005 at the Faculty of Letters of the University of Lisbon)

Antunes, José Freire, *Cartas Particulares a Marcello Caetano*, Vol. 1 (Lisbon: Publicações Dom Quixote, 1985)

Antunes, José Freire, *A Guerra de África – 1961-1974* (Lisbon: Círculo de Leitores, 1995)

Baêna, Luís Sanches de, *Fuzileiros Factos e Feitos na Guerra de África 1961/1974 – Crónica dos Feitos na Guiné* (Comissão Cultural da Marinha, Edições Inapa, 2006)

Bernardo, Manuel A., *Marcello e Spínola: a Ruptura* (Lisbon: Editorial Estampa, 1996)

Bernardo, Manuel A., *Guerra, Paz E ... Fuzilamentos dos Guerreiros; Guiné 1970-1980* (Lisbon: Editora Prefácio, 2007)

Cabral, Luís, *Crónica da Libertação* (Lisbon: O Jornal, 1984)

Cabrita, Felícia, *Massacres em África*, 3ª edição (A esfera dos livros, 2011)

Caetano, Marcello, *O 25 de Abril e o Ultramar – Três entrevistas e alguns depoimentos* (Lisbon: Verbo, (s.d.))

Caetano, Marcello, *Depoimento* (Rio de Janeiro: Distribuidora Record, 1974)

Calheiros, José de Moura, *A última missão* (Lisbon: Caminhos Romanos, 2010)

Calvão, Alpoim, *De Conakry ao M.D.L.P.* (Lisbon: Intervenção, 1976)

Cann, John P., *A Marinha em África, Angola, Guiné e Moçambique Campanhas Fluviais – 1961-1974* (Lisbon: Prefácio, 2009)

Castanheira, José Pedro, *Quem mandou matar Amílcar Cabral* (Lisbon: Relógio de Água Editores, 1995)

CIA Intelligence Report, 'Soviet General Purpose Naval Deployments. Outside Home Waters: Characteristics and Trends' (June 1973)

CIA National Intelligence Survey, 'Guinea' (May 1973)

CIA, 'Impact of Soviet Naval Presence in Third World Countries, Guinea' (January 1983), pp.19-30

Cunha, Silva, *O Ultramar, a Nação e o 25 de Abril* (Coimbra: Atlântida, 1977)

Cunha, Silva, *Ainda o 25 de Abril* (Lisbon: Centro do Livro Brasileiro, 1984)

Diallo, Alpha-Abdoulaye, *La vérité du ministre: Dix ans dans les geôles de Sékou Touré* (Paris: Calmann-Lévy, 1985)

Diallo, Bilguissa, *Guinée, 22 novembre 1970* (Paris: Éditions L'Harmattan, 2014)

jaló, Amadú Bailo, *Guineense Comando Português, Comandos Africanos 1964-1974*, Vol. 1 (Lisbon: Associação de Comandos, 2010)

Eberspacher, Cord & Wiechmann, Gerhard, *Systemkonflikt in Afrika – Deutsch-deutsche Auseinandersetzungen im Kalten Krieg am Beispiel Guineas 1969-1972*, Bd. 23 Nr.23 (2008)

Gomez, Alsény René, *Camp Boiro – Parler ou Périr* (Paris: Éditions L'Harmattan, 2007)

Hernández, Humberto Trujillo, *El Grito del Baobab* (Havana: Editorial de Ciencias Sociales, 2008)

Hinkeldey, Björn, 'La politique allemande de la Guinée vers 1970', *Outre-mers*, tome 98, no. 372–373 (2e semestre 2011), Les deux Allemagnes et l'Afrique, pp.141-144

Hortelão, Rui, Baêna, Luís Sanches de & Sousa, Abel Melo e, *Alpoim Calvão – Honra e Dever – Uma Quase Biografia* (Porto: Editora Caminhos Romanos, 2012)

Kaba 41, Camara, *Dans la Guinée de Sékou Touré: Cela a bien eu lieu* (Paris: Éditions L'Harmattan, 1998)

Keita, Sidiki Kobélé, *La Guinée de Sékou Touré – Pourquoi la prision du camp Boiro?* (Paris: Éditions L'Harmattan, 2014)

Lemos, Mário Matos e, *O 25 de Abril, Uma Síntese, Uma Perspectiva* (Lisbon: Editorial Notícias, 1986)

Lemos, Mário Matos e, *A Invasão de Conakry – Os antecedentes políticos da operação 'Mar Verde'* – Mátria XXI, Centro de Investigação Prof. Doutor Joaquim Veríssimo Serrão (Santarém: 2014)

Lewin, André, *Ahmed Sékou Touré (1922–1984) Président de la Guinée*, Vol. VI (1970-1976) (Paris: Éditions L'Harmattan, 2009)

Lima, Alexandre Coutinho e, *A Retirada de Guileje – A verdade dos factos*, 3rd ed. (DG Edições, 2009)

Lobato, António, *Liberdade ou Evasão*, 2nd ed. (Amadora: Erasmos Editora, 1995)

Mara, Facély II, *Camp Boiro ou le Sixième Continent – Voyage dans les entrailles d'une prison* (Paris: Éditions L'Harmattan, 2018)

Marinho, António Luís, *Operação Mar Verde – Um documento para a história* (Lisbon: Temas e Debates, 2006)

Matos, José, 'O último ano do Fiat G.91 na Guiné', *Revista Militar* no. 4 (April 2020), pp.395-414

Matos, José, 'Into Africa', *Aeroplane* magazine (November 2020), pp.84-89

Medeiros, Gago de, *Um Açoriano no Mundo*, 2 vols (Ponta Delgada: Livraria Martins, 1977)

Nogueira, Alberto Franco, *Salazar, O Último Combate (1964-1970)*, vol. VI (Porto: Civilização Editora, 1985)

Policarpo, Fernando, *Batalhas da História de Portugal, Guerra de África, Guiné, 1963-1974*, vol. 21 (Lisbon: Academia Portuguesa da História, 2006)

Spínola, António, *Portugal e o Futuro*, 5th Ed. (Arcádia, 1974)

Spínola, António, *País Sem Rumo – Contributo para a História de uma Revolução* (Lisbon: SCIRE, 1978)

Resenha Histórico-Militar das Campanhas de África (1961-1974), Estado-Maior do Exército, 5 vols (Lisbon: 1989-2009)

Rittmuller, Adalbert, *Portugal schoß, die DDR gewann, die Bundesrepublik verlor – Die Rolle der DDR beim Abbruch der diplomatischen Beziehungen durch Guinea 1970/71*, Bd. 27 Nr. 27 (2010)

Rosa, António Júlio, *Memórias de um prisioneiro de guerra* (Porto: Edição Campo das Letras, 2003)

Starckmann, Georges, *Noir Canon – Mémoires d'un marchand d'armes* (Paris: Belfond, 1992)

Tíscar, Maria José, *Diplomacia Peninsular e Operações Secretas na Guerra Colonial* (Lisbon: Edições Colibri, 2013)

Tíscar, Maria José, *A Pide no Xadrez Africano – Conversas com o inspector Fragoso Allas*, 2nd ed. (Lisbon: Edições Colibri, 2018)

Thomaz, Américo, *Últimas Décadas de Portugal*, vol. IV (Lisbon: Fernando Pereira, 1983)

Xavier, Leonor, *Rui Patrício – A vida conta-se inteira* (Lisbon: Temas e Debates/Círculo de Leitores, 2010)

Notes

Introduction

1 The Portuguese never admitted any involvement in the operation, which did not prevent the UN Security Council from ordering Portugal to pay for the damage caused in Conakry. However, Sékou Touré, in a letter to the UN Secretary General, refused such compensation, arguing that the only possible compensation was the immediate independence of the Portuguese colonies. See André Lewin, *Ahmed Sékou Touré (1922–1984) Président de la Guinée*, Vol. VI (1970–1976) (Paris: Éditions L'Harmattan, 2009), p.26.

2 Spínola's own affirmation. Cf. AHM – Div. 2, Section 4, Cx. 306, No. 1, reserved No. 114, doc. 217. In the PIDE documentation existing at the National Archives Torre do Tombo, in Lisbon, it was not possible to find any reference to the FLNG (*Front de Libération National de la Guinée)*, although we can imagine that such a process existed, given the contacts maintained with the opponents of Sékou Touré.

3 António Luís Marinho, *Operação Mar Verde – Um documento para a história* (Lisbon: Temas e Debates, 2006).

4 Joaquim Furtado, 'A Guerra', episode 19 (RTP, 2007).

5 Alpoim Calvão, *De Conakry ao MDLP – dossier secreto* (Lisbon: Intervenção, 1976).

6 António Lobato, *Liberdade ou Evasão,* 2nd ed. (Amadora: Erasmos Editora, 1995). See also António Júlio Rosa, *Memórias de um Prisão de Guerra* (Porto: Edição Campo das Letras, 2003).

7 António Vassalo, *Operação Mar Verde* (Porto: Caminhos Romanos, 2012).

8 This opposition movement was created in 1966 and had its headquarters in Abidjan, Côte d'Ivoire. Cf. Facély Mara II, *Camp Boiro or the Sixième Continent – Voyage dans les entrailles d'une prison* (Paris: Éditions L'Harmattan, 2018), p.197. The newspaper *Le Monde,* in its 6 April 1966 edition, reports a Reuters telex about a meeting in Abidjan with several African heads of state who opposed Sékou Touré and the creation of a local section of the National Liberation Front of Guinea (FLNG), of which there were already several sections, especially in Liberia, Sierra Leone, Senegal, Alto Volta (now Burkina Faso) and Niger. The movement seems to have begun that year, with the headquarters established in the capital of Côte d'Ivoire. During this meeting, Lamad Camara, spokesman for the Guineans living in Côte d'Ivoire, underlined the immensity of the task to be carried out to organise the movement and save Guinea from "the domination of a man like Sékou Touré, blinded by the psychosis of imperialism".

9 António Spínola, *País Sem Rumo – Contributo para a História de uma Revolução* (Lisbon: SCIRE, 1978), pp.25–26.

10 Who was then Lieutenant Colonel, and later General, Pedro Cardoso.

11 Luís de Almeida Cabral was the first President of Guinea-Bissau between 1974 and 1980, when he was overthrown by a military coup headed by Nino Vieira.

12 Luís Cabral, *Crónica da Libertação* (Lisbon: Edições 'O Jornal', 1984), p.393.

13 Luís Cabral, 'Prender Spínola', in José Freire Antunes, *A Guerra de África (1961–1974)*, Vol.I (Lisbon: Círculo de Leitores, 1995), p.541.

14 Joaquim Moreira da Silva Cunha was Overseas Minister from 1965–73, and then Defence Minister from 1973–74.

15 Silva J. Cunha, *Ainda o 25 de Abril* (Lisbon: Centro do Livro Brasileiro, 1984), p.95.

16 Silva J. Cunha, *Ainda o 25 de Abril* (Lisbon: Centro do Livro Brasileiro, 1984), p.95.

17 Luís Cabral, 'Prender Spínola', in José Freire Antunes, *A Guerra de África (1961–1974),* Vol. I (Lisbon: Círculo de Leitores, 1995), pp.545–546; Felícia Cabrita, *Massacres em África,* 3rd ed. (Lisbon: A esfera dos livros, 2011), pp.181–210.

18 Cabrita, p.203.

19 Joaquim Furtado, 'A Guerra', episode 18 (RTP, 2007).

20 SHDN – GR9 Q5 122: Special Intelligence Bulletin No. 11.101 of the Secrétariat Général de la Défense Nationale, Paris (27/11/1970).

21 Cord Eberspacher & Gerhard Wiechmann, *Systemkonflikt in Afrika – Deutsch-deutsche Auseinandersetzungen im Kalten Krieg am Beispiel Guineas 1969–1972*, vol. 23 No. 23 (2008), pp.30–41; Adalbert Rittmuller, *Portugal shot, the GDR won, the Federal Republic lost – The role of the GDR in Guinea's severance of diplomatic relations 1970/71*, vol. 27, No. 27 (2010), pp.130–147; Björn Hinkeldey, 'La politique allemande de la Guinée vers 1970', *Outre-mers* 98, no. 372–373 (2e semestre 2011), Les deux Allemagnes et l'Afrique, pp.141–144.

22 Jean-Paul Alata, who was a close collaborator of Sékou Touré until that time and who would later be arrested and accused of conspiring with the Portuguese, describes in his book *Prisão de África* (Edição Livros do Brasil) the atmosphere at that time and the repression carried out by the regime after the invasion.

23 Alpha-Abdoulaye Diallo, in *La vérité du ministre: Dix ans dans les geôles de Sékou Touré* (Paris: Calmann-Lévy, 1985), p.7, tells that he was prisoner number 2,569, but that the true number of Guineans imprisoned during the repression was unknown. The revolutionary court sentenced 62 people to death and issued 68 life sentences. Cf. Marinho, p.168; Rittmuller, p.145. Alsény René Gomez in *Camp Boiro – Parler or Périr* (Paris: Éditions L'Harmattan, 2007), p.200, states that the total number of prisoners at Camp Boiro was 680.

24 Thierno Ibrahima Diallo was a former officer of the French colonial army who joined the FLNG and, due to his military experience, became the chief of the military branch of the organisation.

25 Bilguissa Diallo, *Guinea, 22 November 1970* (Paris: Éditions L'Harmattan, 2014).

26 Alpha-Abdoulaye Diallo, *La vérité du ministre: Dix ans dans les geôles de Sékou Touré* (Paris: Calmann-Lévy, 1985).

27 Pascal Airault & Jean-Pierre Bat, *Françafrique: Opérations secrètes et affaires d'Etat* (Paris: Éditions Tallandier, 2018), pp.59–65.

28 Rittmuller, pp.130–147.

29 https://savoirs.rfi.fr/fr/2-mar-verde-et-lannee-de-la-grande-purge.

30 Mémoire Collective, a plural history of political violence in Guinea: https://www.memoire-collective-guinee.org/Memoire-collective.pdf.

31 This work is the only biography that exists about Calvão and was published by Editorial Caminhos Romanos in 2012.

Chapter 1

1 Suzanne Cronje, 'Portuguese Guinea Hit Hard by African Rebels', *The Washington Post* (22 February 1968).

2 Arnaldo Schultz, an officer in the Portuguese Army, was Minister of the Interior from 1958–1961. After a brief stint in Angola in 1963, he was appointed to Guinea.

3 José Pedro Castanheira, 'Ao serviço de Spínola e Marcelo', *'Expresso – Revista'* no 1299 (20 September 1997), p.56. This version of Schultz's departure from Guinea is not confirmed by other sources, although the military situation was not really favourable to Portuguese forces at that time.

4 Manuel Gomes de Araújo, an army officer, was Under-secretary of State for War from 1942–47. Before becoming Minister of Defence, he was Chief of Staff of the Armed Forces (CEMGFA) in 1961 and 1962 when Salazar was Minister of Defence. He was then appointed Minister of Defence from 1962–68.

5 Silva Cunha, *Ainda o 25 de Abril* (CLB, 1984), p.92.

6 Testimony of António de Spínola in *Os Últimos Governadores do Império* (Lisbon: Edições Neptuno, 1994), pp.63–65; António de Spínola, *País sem Rumo: Contributo para a História de uma Revolução* (SCIRE, 1978), pp.22–23.

7 ADN – CEMGFA/017/0034/006.

8 This letter, dated 11 August 1966, presents a very lucid analysis of the difficulties faced by Portuguese forces in Guinea and their inability to dominate the guerrilla movement. Cf. ADN – SGDN/2REP/106/0411/008.

9 ADN – CEMGFA/017/0034/006: O problema militar da Guiné – Anexo A.

10 This new strategy was outlined in a series of Chief Command directives for troops in Guinea.

11 ADN – SGDN/2REP/78/329/3: CCFAG Directiva No 65/6. This Chief Command directive is a good example of the new policy in Guinea.

12 Cabrita, p.201. Felícia Cabrita describes in her book the atmosphere in Chão Manjaco, with the population convinced that the war was over. The guerrillas participated in the hoax in order to capture Spínola, and when he did not appear at the meeting on 20 April, they decided to eliminate the majors. In a letter he wrote to the Minister of Defence on 21 April 1970, Spínola acknowledged that the death of these officers "was a hard blow that we suffered, as they were a team of exceptional value and determination". Cf. ADN – GABMIN/007/0029/004.

13 Joaquim Furtado, 'A Guerra', Episode 18 (RTP, 2007).

14 Manuel Belchior, *Os Congressos do Povo na Guiné* (Arcadia, 1973). Manuel Belchior was Spínola's special adviser at these events, to which he dedicated himself with enthusiasm.

15 Otelo Saraiva de Carvalho, *Alvorada em Abril* (Amadora: Livraria Bertrand, 1977), p. 86.

16 Otelo Saraiva de Carvalho, *Alvorada em Abril* (Amadora: Livraria Bertrand, 1977), p. 86.

17 Otelo Saraiva de Carvalho, *Alvorada em Abril* (Amadora: Livraria Bertrand, 1977), p. 86. Otelo Saraiva de Carvalho describes the fear that the visits of Spínola provoked in the commanders of the units, which were always distressed by the visits of the general.

18 AHPR – GB/GB0205/1729/009.

19 ADN SGDN/2REP/096/0384/015: Sitrep Circunstanciado no 31/68 do COMZAVERDEGUINE, Bissau (31/7/1968). This jet was shot down by fire from a DShK 12.7mm heavy machine gun. The pilot, Lieutenant Colone; Costa Gomes, ejected safely and was recovered.

20 AHPR – GB/GB0205/1729/009.

21 AHPR – GB/GB0205/1729/009.

22 AHPR – GB/GB0205/1729/009.

23 ADN – CEMGFA/017/0034/006.

24 Venâncio Augusto Deslandes, an aeronautics officer, held several posts during the *Estado Novo* (2nd Portuguese Republic), such as Deputy Undersecretary of State for Defence and Portuguese ambassador in Madrid. He was also governor and commander-in-chief of Angola at the start of the colonial war and was dismissed in 1962 due to a disagreement with the Overseas Minister, Adriano Moreira. Between 1968 and 1972 he was CEMGFA, later replaced by Costa Gomes.

25 ADN – CEMGFA/017/0036/024.

26 Meeting in the Council Presidency on 19 May 1969 reproduced in António Luís Marinho, *Operação Mar Verde – Um documento para a história* (Lisbon: Temas e Debates, 2006), pp.216–220.

27 ADN – CEMGFA/017/0037/044.

28 ADN – SGDN/2REP/88/364/24: SUPINTREP No 35 of CCFAG.

29 Aristides Peraira, *O meu testemunho, uma luta, um partido, dois países*, Documented version (Lisbon: Editorial Notícias, 2003), p.195.

30 Aristides Maria Pereira was, together with Amílcar Cabral, founder of the PAIGC and one of the most important guerrilla leaders. After Cabral's death he assumed the party presidency until Guinea-Bissau's independence in 1974. After that he would leave Guinea, being the first President of Cape Verde.

31 Aristides Peraira, *O meu testemunho, uma luta, um partido, dois países*, Documented version (Lisbon: Editorial Notícias, 2003), p.192. Sweden was always an important supporter of the PAIGC in Europe, and Amílcar Cabral was always well received in Stockholm. Although they did not offer military support, the Swedes provided political and humanitarian coverage for the PAIGC.

32 ADN – CEMGFA/017/0036/028.

33 SHDN – GR9 Q5 122: Information Note No 10 175 of the Secrétariat Général de la Défense Nationale – Senegal and the Problem of Portuguese Guinea, Paris (19/2/1970).

34 SHDN – GR9 Q5 122: Monthly Bulletin No 116. From 23 February 1970 to 17 March 1970.

35 Horácio de Sá Viana Rebelo, an Army general, was Governor of Angola between 1957 and 1960. He became Minister of Defence with Marcello Caetano's assumption of power in 1968.

36 AHPR – GB/GB0205/1729/035.

37 ADN – GABMIN/007/0029/004.

38 This was the impression that Marcello Caetano had about the Senegalese president. In Caetano's opinion, the Senegalese forces were not strong enough to contain the PAIGC, and therefore Senghor could not control the guerrillas in his country. However, it should be remembered that the Senegalese leader had signed an agreement with Cabral's party in March 1966 which gave a number of facilities to the guerrillas on Senegalese territory. Cf. SHDN – GR9 Q5 122: Protocol of agreement between Senegal and the PAIGC of 21 March 1966.

39 AHPR – GB/GB0205/1729/041.

40 AHPR – GB/GB0205/1729/009.

41 ADN – GABMIN/007/0029/004.

42 ADN – GABMIN/007/0029/004.

43 José Freire Antunes, *Cartas Particulares a Marcello Caetano*, Vol. I (Lisbon: D. Quixote Publications, 1985), p.149.

44 Marinho, p.88.

45 In 1996, Alpoim Calvão told the RTP TV programme *Enviado Especial* that he had told Marcello Caetano that he did not know what the outcome of the coup would be, but that he hoped at least to bring away the Portuguese prisoners. Marcello said that if the operation had been for this purpose alone it would have been worthwhile and gave his support. https://arquivos.rtp.pt/conteudos/operacao-mar-verde-parte-i/.

Chapter 2

1 Alpoim Calvão had already successfully commanded the operations that had led to the destruction of two PAIGC boats – *Bandim* and *Patrice Lumumba*. John P. Cann, in his book *The Navy in Africa*, pp.288–289, writes: "If the interdiction operations had been successful in the border area, why not extend them to Conakry herself, since a raid on this site would have the potential to destroy the entire PAIGC fleet. The Marines had proved capable of successfully conducting local incursions and therefore, with some imagination and careful planning, a long-distance attack on Conakry was a realistic possibility."

2 Semanário *Sol*, Lisbon, 9 March 2012.

3 He was the Commander of Maritime Defence in Guinea.

4 BCM-AH – COLOREDO-Guiné Fund, Pasta 47: Operation Green Sea – Preparation (n.a.). The type of magnetic limpet naval mine to be used in the operation had been invented during the First World War and clung to the hull of a ship, with a timer that allowed the programming of its detonation. Portugal did not have these mines in its arsenal, which led Calvão to travel to South Africa to obtain them.

5 ADN – SGDN/2REP/088/0363/013. SUPINTREP 1/68 do EMA: Forças navais do inimigo. República da Guiné e PAIGC (29/2/1968).

6 ADN – SGDN/2REP/106/0412/011. By the end of 1967, news emerged that the Russians had warned Amílcar Cabral that if the ships came to Guinea and were seized by the Portuguese, the Russians and Cubans would no longer provide military equipment to the PAIGC. See ADN – SGDN/2REP/100/0394/028.

7 Calvão, pp.64–65.

8 These talks took place in Bissau from 29 July to 6 August 1966 and received a favourable opinion from the authorities in Lisbon. Cf. ADN – SGDN/2REP/106/0411/008.

9 These requests are contained in an August 1966 report of the FLNG, in which the organisation asks for facilities for the entry and transit of FLNG members to Guinea; the establishment of an office in Bissau; support for training FLNG members; financial support, armaments and other material means. See ADN – SGDN/2REP/106/0411/008.

10 AHM – Div. 2, etc. It was written, at the request of the then director of the Military History Commission, General Manuel Freire Themudo Barata, on 4 January 1989, under the title *Subsidy for the clarification of the 'Operation Green Sea' held at the TO* [Theatre of Operations] *in Guinea in November 1970*. This statement, 11 typed sheets in response to various questions, was intended to clarify the text prepared for the *Historical-Military Review of the African Campaigns (1961–1974)*.

11 One of the "25 essential objectives" of the operation was "the murder of Amílcar Cabral", which, as seen above, Spínola denied: arrested, yes; killed, no. Cf. Fernando Policarpo, *Batalhas da História de Portugal – A Guerra em África – Guiné, 1963–1974* (Academia Portuguesa de História), p.98.

12 It is not clear whether General Spínola understood that having Amílcar Cabral imprisoned in Bissau would facilitate an understanding with the PAIGC leadership or whether he thought Cabral would be at their side in the manoeuvre to conduct the ongoing political-military process. Nor is it clear what interest this would have if the coup d'état triumphed, since in that case the winners guaranteed that they would expel the PAIGC. The truth is that Alpoim Calvão, in an interview with the Lisbon daily newspaper *Público* on 21 May 1991, stated that if Amílcar Cabral were in Conakry and captured "he would be eliminated or [made] a prisoner; but more certainly eliminated. After all, was Cabral's murder not out of the question? Or of other leaders?"

13 Alexandre Ribeiro da Cunha (1915–83) was Salazar's secretary (1939–50), and was then placed in the Ministry of Corporations, having represented Portugal at the Bureau International du Travail (BIT) in Geneva, hence his knowledge of Mr Doré of the FLNG. A respected personality, he was Senior Inspector of the Office of Political Affairs at the Ministry of Overseas Territories. In that capacity he was in Dakar in 1967, with PIDE Inspector Matos Rodrigues, for exploratory talks with a Senegalese delegation with a view to the mediation of Senegal in order to reach an understanding between the Portuguese government and the PAIGC.

14 ANTT – AOS/CO/UL 52, docs. 626–627.

15 David Soumah was a well-known Guinean trade unionist who had disagreed with Sékou Touré even before Guinea-Conakry's independence. In 1956 he left the country and ended up in exile in Dakar, Senegal. In 1970 he was in Lisbon, where he was supervised by the Portuguese authorities. Diallo, *Guinée, 22 November 1970,* p.29; Marinho, p.70.

16 ANTT – AOS/CO/UL 52, doc. 648.

17 AOS/CO/UL 52, doc. 663. This information was seen by Salazar, who crossed out 'Top Secret' and wrote 'Secret', 'Seen' and the date 22.8.1968 instead. By this date, Salazar had already suffered his fall in Estoril and was only two weeks away from being interned. However, during that month (3 August – 4 September) he had maintained his usual activity. Cf. Franco Nogueira, vol. VI, pp.376–384.

18 ANTT – AOS/CO/UL 52, docs. 664–667.

19 Gonçalo Luís Maravilhas Correia Caldeira Coelho (1918–95). He was interim Director General of Political Affairs in the Ministry of Foreign Affairs between 15 January and 10 December 1968, the date on which he took full office, which he held until 1973.

20 Highlights of Salazar.

21 ANTT – AOS/CO/ UL 52, docs. 658–682.

22 Created on 26 March 1966 by Guinean expatriates in Côte d'Ivoire, which was later joined "by almost all Guinean exiles in Europe and Africa", according to the author of the 'Note'.

23 Sékou Touré clearly accused the French and German special services of complicity in landing.

24 A card from Silva Cunha to Salazar tells us that this report ("to which I ask you to give your attention", he writes) was delivered "to the police". Cf. AOS/CO/UL 52, doc. 662.

25 AOS/CO/UL 56, pp. 554–556.

26 According to António Luís Marinho, the Minister of Defence, General Viana Rebelo, also did not agree with the operation.

27 This communication had also been transmitted to the Ministry of Overseas Territories. See ADN – SGDN/2REP/106/0411/008.

28 ADN – GABMIN/007/0029/005: Information on a meeting with FLNG (10/12/69).

29 Agostinho Barbieri Baptista Cardoso (1907–85).

30 However, in the PIDE/DGS archive at Torre do Tombo it was not possible to find any information related to this operation.

31 According to a journalist from the weekly *Jeune Afrique*, Bruno Crimi – quoted by Leopoldo Amado in his book *Guerra Colonial e Guerra de Libertação Nacional*, pp.300–302 – PIDE Inspector Ernesto Lopes Ramos was in contact with the German Federal Intelligence Service (*Bundes Nachrich Dienst*, BND) and was a German secret agent, posted at the Embassy of the Federal Republic of Germany in Conakry, to collect, through an official of the Presidency of the Guinean Republic, "the information that should ensure the success of the operation". However, we have to treat this information with some reservation, given the fact that everything indicates that there was no collaboration between the BND and Calvão.

32 AHU – MU/GM/GNP/069.

33 AHU – MU/GM/GNP/069.

34 'Belle Vue'.

35 Luís Cabral, Amílcar's brother, said that "contrary to what happened at weekends" (21 November was Saturday), the President (Touré) was not at his Belle Vue house, which seems to indicate that the information was correct and the action failed by chance. Cf. *Crónica da Libertação*, pp.359–360.

36 Calvão, p.68. In the book he wrote in 1976, Calvão mentions that Spínola did indeed intend to install an FLNG guerrilla movement in Guinea, and that this hypothesis was considered in October 1969. He also says that it was he who proposed to Spínola the idea of a *coup d'état* in Conakry. But in an interview he gave to Manuel Amaro Bernardo, he says that when he visited General Spínola in August 1969, during the period in which he was on holiday in Portugal, to discuss the possibility of an operation to sabotage PAIGC ships, Spínola told him of the existence of the FLNG and of the contacts that this entity had been maintaining with the Ministry of Overseas Territories for a long time, and that it was Spínola who came up with the idea of taking advantage of the FLNG to overthrow the Guinean dictator's regime. What is strange is that a month after this meeting, Calvão went to Pretoria to pick up the limpet mines, maintaining his intention to carry out the sabotage operation, as if the hypothesis of a coup d'état had not been considered. Cf. Manuel A. Bernardo, *Guerra, Paz E.. Fuzilamentos dos Guerreiros; Guiné 1970–1980* (Lisbon: Prefácio, 2007), p.274.

37 Matos Rodrigues was the PIDE inspector in Guinea in charge of intelligence. He would be replaced shortly after the failure of the operation by the Fragoso Allas inspector.

38 Diallo, *Guinée, 22 Novembre 1970,* pp.131–137.

39 The report shows that Diallo was self-employed in the recruitment of activists and that he took full responsibility towards the Senegalese authorities. In fact, Diallo was cut off from relations with Soumah, but worked on recruitment, with money also provided by the Portuguese authorities. Cf. Diallo, *Guinée, 22 Novembre 1970,* p.87.

40 Camara Laye was a Guinean writer who held important positions in Conakry in the Ministry of Information, before going into exile in Dakar dissatisfied with the regime of Sékou Touré.

41 Diallo, *Guinée, 22 Novembre 1970,* p.89. Another incident mentioned in the report was the arrest in the Gambia of Mamadou Samba Diallo, who would eventually confess to recruiting Guineans for a military operation against Sékou Touré.

42 ADN – GABMIN/007/0029/005: Report – Talk with Jean Marie Doré, (24/3/70). It seems clear that Senghor knew that the FLNG was based in Dakar.

43 Diallo, *Guinée, 22 Novembre 1970,* pp.85–86. This meeting in Abidjan was eventually denounced by a member of the FLNG who had contacts with the ambassador of Guinea-Conakry in Senegal. See pp.86–87.

44 Suzanne Cronje, 'Opposition to Toure Regime Reported in Nearby Nations', *The Washington Post* (24/11/1970).

45 Antunes, *Cartas Particulares a Marcello Caetano*, pp.148–150.

46 Certainly David Soumah.

47 AHU – MU/GM/GNP/069.

48 Antunes, *Cartas Particulares a Marcello Caetano*, p.223.

49 Between December 1970 and July 1971, the area of operation of this force was off the coast of Portuguese Guinea, in a clear move to stop further attacks directed against the Republic of Guinea by sea. From September 1971, the Soviet naval force concentrated near Conakry, in protection of Touré and against his internal opponents. Tactically, the protection of Touré was a defensive operation, but at the strategic level it went much further, as it would allow the PAIGC to continue its actions without fear of attacks by sea. Cf. Mário Matos e Lemos, *O 25 de Abril, Uma Síntese, Uma Perspectiva* (Lisbon: Editorial Notícias, 1986).

Chapter 3

1 BCM-AH – COLOREDO Fundo – Guinea, folder 47: Operation Mar Verde – Preparation (n.a.). LFG *Orion*, commanded by Faria dos Santos, was the main vessel used to collect and transport the Guineans to the island of Soga.

2 Calvão, p.69.

3 Calvão, pp.65–66.

4 Calvão, p.70.

5 Calvão, p.71.

6 André Lewin quotes Pierre Henri Clostermann, a former French pilot and deputy, who in his memoirs says that he brought from Paris high-resolution aerial photos of Conakry and gave them to the Portuguese. However, there is no certainty about this information. Cf. Lewin, pp.56–58.

7 Marinho, pp.78–80.

8 Georges Starckmann, *Noir Canon – Mémoires d'un marchand d'armes* (Paris: Belfond, 1992), p.131.

9 Georges Starckmann, *Noir Canon – Mémoires d'un marchand d'armes* (Paris: Belfond, 1992), p.133.

10 Georges Starckmann, *Noir Canon – Mémoires d'un marchand d'armes* (Paris: Belfond, 1992), p.133.

11 David Soumah was a well-known Guinean trade unionist who had disagreed with Sékou Touré even before Guinea-Conakry's independence. In 1956, he left the country and ended up in exile in Dakar, Senegal. In 1970, he was in Lisbon, where he was supervised by the Portuguese authorities. Diallo, *Guinée, 22 November 1970,* p.29; Marinho, p.70.

12 Diallo, *Guinée, 22 Novembre 1970,* pp.93–94.

13 In an interview with Sidiki Kobélé Keita in 2004, Calvão justified the choice because David Soumah did not deserve his confidence and was a civilian who was not prepared for a military operation. Cf. Sidiki Kobélé Keita, *La Guinée de Sékou Touré – Pourquoi la prision du camp Boiro?* (Paris: Éditions L'Harmattan, 2014), p.284.

14 Calvão, p.71.

15 Operations Order for Operation *Green Sea*. Cf. Marinho, pp.247–248. See also José Manuel Barroso's article in the *Diário de Notícias* of 22 November 2000 on the 30th anniversary of the operation.

16 The African commandos coming from Fá Mandinga by boat arrived on the island of Soga on 17 November, without knowing anything about the operation. In order to not compromise the secrecy of the operation, both commandos and marines remained on the transport boats, prevented from going ashore and contacting the forces stationed on the island. See Amadú Bailo Djaló, *Guineense Comando Português, Comandos Africanos 1964–1974*, Vol. I (Lisbon: Associação de Comandos, 2010), p.170.

17 Diallo arrived in Bissau on 20 November, because on that day he went with General Spínola to the island of Soga.

18 Calvão, p.72. It seems that the commandos became aware of the operation on 18 November and immediately expressed reservations about the military incursion into Conakry. Major Leal da Almeida even sent a message to Alpoim Calvão that the commando company refused to participate in the mission. On that day, he was taken by Calvão to Bissau, where General Spínola convinced him to participate. He returned on 19 November. Cf. Djaló, pp.173–174.

19 Marinho, pp.90–95.

20 Marinho, pp.96–97. Calvão, p.73.

21 Calvão, pp.74–81; Marinho, pp.108–133.

22 According to Sidiki Kobélé Keita, it was Thierno Diallo, Hassan Assad and Siradiou Diallo who convinced the Portuguese authorities that David Soumah could not be trusted and that he should not participate in the Conakry expedition. Cf. Keita, p.152.

23 José Matos, 'Into Africa', *Aeroplane* magazine (November 2020), pp. 84–89.

24 It was not possible to determine the exact number of military personnel on board. Thierno Diallo in his report on the operation speaks of about 200 men and seems to refer to all the military personnel who were effectively involved in the invasion. It should be noted that the FLNG dissidents did not all board the boats, but only a selected group that would be mainly on board the *Montante* and *Bombarda* LDGs and would not be more than 100 men. See ADN – GABMIN/007/0029/005: Report presented by Commander Diallo Thierno on Operation 22/11/1970, (25/11/1970). António Luís Marinho, in *Operation Mar Verde – A document for history,* pp.85–86, states that the DFE would be 80 men plus 150 from the C.C. Africanos, which together with elements of the FLNG gives about 330 men.

25 Calvão, p.73.

26 Calvão, p.76. Mission report to Victor group in Marinho, pp.267–269. In the 2nd division of the SGDN in the ADN, it is possible to easily find, based on a research on the naval means of the PAIGC, the information board that the Portuguese authorities had regarding these means. The PAIGC ships were listed since 1967 as probably being P-6 torpedo boats, although lacking torpedo capacity due to the absence of launch tubes. Very similar to the PAIGC P-6s were the Komar boats that had, instead of torpedoes, two anti-ship missile launchers for P-15 Termit missiles (SS-N-2 Styx). The Komars had been supplied to the Guinean Navy and were in Conakry along with the P-6s, when they were destroyed by the Rebordão de Brito group.

27 BCM-AH – COLOREDO Fund – Guinea, folder 47: Operation Mar Verde – Report of the Commander (s.d.); Marinho, pp.110–111. Calvão, p.78.

28 See the report of the mission in Marinho, pp.274–276. Calvão, pp.78–79.

29 Alsény René Gomez in *Camp Boiro – Parler or Périr* (Paris: Éditions L'Harmattan, 2007), p.37, states that 76 detainees were released, but Alpoim Calvão speaks of 400 political prisoners, which is certainly an exaggeration.

30 Marinho, p.115.

31 Diallo, *La verité du ministre* p.24.

32 According to Calvão (p.78), the camp was handed over to the FLNG forces (20 men) in the person of Barry Ibrahima, who was at the time Minister for Financial Control. This leader would be sentenced to death and was one of those hanged from the Tombo bridge. However, Alpha

Diallo also reports that Ibrahima was present at the presidential palace that early morning with Sékou Touré. Diallo, *La Vérité du Ministre,* p.17.

33 In an interview he gave to Manuel Amaro Bernardo (see *Guerra, Paz e Fuzilamentos dos Guerreiros*, p.235), Marcelino da Mata confirms that he killed 94 soldiers, but that the real number of dead would have been higher than that.

34 Calvão, p.77; Marinho, pp.121–122.

35 Marinho, p.123; Rittmuller, pp.141–142. Another collateral victim of the invasion would be the deputy ambassador of the German Democratic Republic (GDR), Siegfried Krebs, 35, who would be killed on his way from his flat to the embassy. Cf. Eberspacher & Wiechmann, p.33.

36 Report of the Detachment of Special Marines No. 21 in Marinho, pp.260–263.

37 ADN – GABMIN/007/0029/005: 587/70 GAB.

38 Luís Cabral maintains that the radio station attack failed due to the strong resistance there of the PAIGC military. According to Cabral, it would have been the Navy commander, Mateus Correia, with some of the party's combatants, who prevented the takeover of the radio station by invading forces. See Luís Cabral's statement in Joaquim Furtado, 'A Guerra', *Episódio* 19, RTP (2007). Cabral, p.360. Jean-Paul Alata states in this regard that it was the Cuban troops who were stationed near the radio station that defended the installations and not the PAIGC, which according to Alata did nothing. Cf. Anne Blancard, 'Interview with Jean-Paul Alata', *Politique Africaine* (1977).

39 In his report on the operation, Calvão is surprised that the radio station was not taken, as it was only 100 metres from the landing site of the group from LDG *Bombarda*. It seems that Jamanca's team was inexplicably immobile on the beach, thus failing in its objective. The team was carrying an engineer from the FLNG, Tidiane Diallo, who had studied in France and had not been to Conakry for several years. When he arrived on the scene he was disoriented by the building he saw, which he did not recognise as being that of the radio station. Cf. testimony of Amadou Djaló in Joaquim, 'A Guerra', Episode 19, RTP (2007). Djaló, p.181.

40 There was a statement written in French to be read on the radio, but its whereabouts and content are unknown. This statement was in the possession of Alpoim Calvão but was apparently unknown among the main leaders of the FLNG, since Diallo never made any reference to it.

41 Marinho, pp.134–136.

42 Alpoim Calvão reports that the aim was to arrest Cabral, but on the approach to the house there was resistance from the guards defending the PAIGC secretariat facilities and the attackers responded with light weapons and grenade launchers. Cf. Alpoim Calvão's statement in Joaquim Furtado, 'A Guerra', *Episódio* 19, RTP (2007); Calvão, p.77.

43 Statement by Ana Maria Cabral in Joaquim Furtado, 'A Guerra', Episode 19, RTP (2007). Even if Cabral was at home, it was likely that he had also escaped together with his wife, making his capture impossible.

44 ADN – GABMIN/007/0029/005: 589/70 GAB.

45 Relying on information from the French National Defence General Secretariat, the Guineans had received from Moscow between 1966 and 1968 nine MiG-17 fighters, three helicopters and four Yakovlev Yak-18 training aircraft; however, a large proportion of these aircraft were inoperative by the end of 1970. Cf. SHDN – GR9 Q5 122: File No. 52 of the Secrétariat Général de la Défense Nationale, Paris (21/7/1971).

46 Calvão, p.80.

47 It was a group of African commandos (about 20 men) who deserted with Lieutenant Januário Lopes. This African force officer did not agree with the operation and ended up deserting with several members of the group on his way to the airport. Cf. testimony of Amadou Djaló in Joaquim Furtado, 'A Guerra', Episode 19, RTP (2007). Djaló, p.177.

48 Calvão, p.81.

49 BCM-AH – COLOREDO Fund – Guinea, folder 47: Operation Mar Verde – Report of the Commander (s.d.); Marinho, pp.132–133.

50 ADN – GABMIN/007/0029/005: 591/70 GAB.

51 Alpha Abdoulaye Diallo was one of Sékou Touré's closest collaborators, successively holding the posts of Secretary of State for Foreign Affairs, head of the Guinean delegation to the UN and Secretary of State for Youth, Sport and Popular Culture, a position he held when the 1970 invasion took place. During the attack, he was one of the members of the government who went to the presidential palace to organise the security of the head of state and his family. Surprisingly, he was arrested a year later and accused of participating in the conspiracy. He would end up serving a 10-year prison sentence at Camp Boiro.

52 Alpha-Abdoulaye Diallo, *La vérité du ministre: Dix ans dans les jaques de Sékou Touré* (Paris: Calmann-Lévy, 1985), p.19.

53 Alpha-Abdoulaye Diallo, *La vérité du ministre: Dix ans dans les jaques de Sékou Touré* (Paris: Calmann-Lévy, 1985), p.19.

54 Humberto Trujillo Hernández, *El Grito del Baobab* (Havana: Editorial de Ciencias Sociales, 2008), p.95.

55 Humberto Trujillo Hernández, *El Grito del Baobab* (Havana: Editorial de Ciencias Sociales, 2008), p.223.

56 Marinho, p.142.

57 Calvão, p.75. It is interesting to note that over the years the threat of the Guinean MiGs has always been viewed from the Portuguese side with great concern, given the possibility of an attack against Bissau.

58 Calvão, in Antunes, *op. cit.*

59 When the dictator was woken at 0200 hours by some officers who had gone to the presidential palace, Sékou Touré thought that it was a coup d'état and that these officers were there to arrest or eliminate him. Cf. Diallo, *La vérité du ministre,* p.23. This story is repeated by Alsény René Gomez in *Camp Boiro – Parler or Périr*, p.36. However, this version is contested by Sidiki Kobélé Keita in *La Guinée de Sékou Touré – Pourquoi la prision du camp Boiro?* pp.179–181.

60 Suzanne Cronje, 'Opposition to Toure Regime Reported in Nearby Nations', *The Washington Post* (24/11/1970).

61 Born in Brazil, Jean Schramme was managing a plantation in the Belgian Congo when the colony became independent from Belgium in 1960. After independence, he was involved in the Katanga uprising and returned to Belgium in 1968 after his defeat against Congo troops. At the time of the invasion he was in Portugal.

62 Facély II Mara, in his book *Camp Boiro or the Sixième Continent – Voyage dans les entrailles d'une prison* (Paris: Éditions L'Harmattan, 2018), pp.48–49, gives several examples of Sékou Touré's public interventions, where he seems to know clearly the preparation of the invasion, based on the information he had received from neighbouring countries.

63 Camara Kaba 41, *Dans la Guinée de Sékou Touré: Cela a bien eu lieu* (Paris: Éditions L'Harmattan, 1998), p.106. The option of concentrating defence logistics on Samory proved to be a mistake, as Mike team from LDG *Montante* took this position and then ambushed the troops who went to the barracks. Cf. Kaba 41, p.111.

64 Diallo, *The Minister's Truth,* p.14.

65 Diallo, *The Minister's Truth,* p.14.

66 Calvão, p.80. This team was led by Furriel Talabio Djaló, and when one of the FLNG members who was in the group arrived at the palace he was wounded during an exchange of fire with the guards. When they returned to the boarding point, the attack force had already boarded and the group was attacked by the Guinean military, with only two soldiers escaping, who fled by swimming. Cf. Djaló, p.178.

67 Camara Kaba said that many of these prisoners voluntarily surrendered again to Sékou Touré, who showed no mercy in having several of them executed. Cf. Kaba 41, p.111.

68 Calvão, in Antunes, p.515.

69 Lobato, pp.37–39.

70 Lobato, pp.174–175.

71 Lobato heard the fighters take off a few days earlier but realised that they did not return to the city.

72 Marinho, p.141.

73 Calvão, p.83; Marinho, p.142.

74 Lobato, p.176; Calvão, p.83.

75 Djaló, p.182.

76 In an interview with António Luís Marinho, Amadou Djaló said that these men had come with them from Conakry and that they thought that the comrades who had stayed in the capital had seized power, so they went to the north of the country to continue the rebellion. However,

it is strange that these members of the FLNG, who had also been in the capital, thought that the coup had been successful. Cf. Marinho, p.153. The attacks in the Koundara area occurred between 26 and 27 November. Cf. André Lewin, *Ahmed Sékou Touré (1922–1984) – Président de la Guinée,* Vol. VI (Paris: Éditions L'Harmattan, 2009), p.18. According to French sources, this group comprised 150 men, 50 of whom were killed and the rest taken prisoner. Cf. SHDN – GR9 Q5 122: Special Intelligence Bulletin No. 11.126 of the Secrétariat Général de la Défense Nationale, Paris (4/12/1970). On this subject, Sidiki Kobélé Keita mentions that 23 members of the FLNG were captured, 21 of whom were former soldiers of the French colonial army who had come from Senegal and France. Some had taken part in the attack on Conakry but went north in the hope of profiting from the surprise effect. Cf. Keita, p.160. Luciano de Bastos, commander of the Maritime Defence of Guinea, states in his personal diary that there were about 80 men who had come with Calva de Conakry. Cf. Marinho, p.153.

77 Marinho, p.156.

78 ADN – GABMIN/007/0029/005: Travel Report to Guinea (27/11/1970). Lieutenant Colonel Salazar Braga of the Portuguese Army who went from Lisbon to Guinea lists in his report 24 military personnel who had stayed in Bissau, with four other individuals accused of being traitors, which resulted in 28 Portuguese people being released. However, an analysis of other documents in the DNA shows that 24 military personnel went to Lisbon on the Air Force plane, with no reference to anyone having been detained in Bissau. See ADN – SGDN/2REP/102/397/6. However, in a letter from Spínola, dated 26 November 1970, addressed to the Minister of Defence, the Governor mentions that of the 26 prisoners recovered, one defected soldier and one European civilian remained in Bissau. Cf. ADN – GABMIN/007/0029/004.

79 Marinho, p.154.

80 Marinho, pp.156–157.

81 Amadú Djaló says that before embarking on the island of Soga, he received orders from Major Leal de Almeida that the command force should remain in Conakry until the FLNG had the situation under control. Cf. Djaló, p.176.

82 Jean-Paul Alata, *Prisão de África* (Lisbon: Edição Livros do Brasil), p.59.

83 Kaba 41, p.107.

84 Kaba 41, p.107.

85 Facély II Mara, *Camp Boiro or le Sixième Continent – Voyage dans les entrailles d'une prison* (Paris: Éditions L'Harmattan, 2018), p.51. This version is contradicted by Sidiki Kobélé Keita, according to whom the keys to Alpha Yaya's arsenal were with Sergeant Dobo Sovogui, chief of weapons at the time of the attack, and not with President Sékou Touré. The story seems to be confirmed by Dobo Sovogui himself in a radio interview with *Evasion* on 5 December 2016. Cf. https://www.guinee7.com/analyse-des-ragots-sur-lagression-du-22-novembre-1970-et-reflexions-sur-le-rapport-et-les-recommandations-du-cprn-par-sidiki-kobele-keita/.

86 SHDN – GR9 Q5 122: Note No 10 388 of the Secrétariat Général de la Défense Nationale – The Guinean armed forces, Paris (17/4/1970).

87 In Sitrep 46/70 of Comzaverde there is reference to two flights of the Fiat G.91 on a RFOT mission at the southern border in mid-November. See ADN – SGDN/2REP/094/0376/039.

88 Calvão, p.73. The aviation attack was scheduled for 0600 hours, as soon as news of the success of the operation was received in Bissau. Nineteen objectives were planned at the border. Cf. Marinho, pp.138, 171.

89 ADN – GABMIN/007/0029/005: Report presented by Commander Thierno Diallo on Operation 22/11/1970 (25/11/1970).

90 The report presented by Thierno Diallo shows the differences between the Guinean commander and the operations plan, which were demonstrated by Spínola on the island of Soga.

91 BCM-AH – COLOREDO Fund – Guinea, folder 47: Operation Mar Verde – Commander's report (s.d.)

92 José Pedro Castaneira, *O Pide que invadiu Conakry,* in 'Expresso – Revista', no. 1108 (22 January 1994), p.44.

93 Alata, p.60.

94 Calvão, in Antunes, *op cit.*, p.516.

95 Keita, p.285.

96 Calvão, p.103; ADN – SGDN/2REP/74/320/28. In this documental background there is a collection of documents (300+ pages) on the 'Sea Dragon' plan and the information that has been collected.

97 Calvão, p.103. In 1973, the 'Dragão Marinho' suffered a cut in the budget requested and Calvão decided to leave the network and move to the 2nd Division of the General Secretariat of National Defence, where the process with the information gathered is currently located.

98 Leonor Xavier, *Rui Patrício – A vida se conta inteira* (Lisbon: Temas e Debates/Círculo de Leitores, 2010), p.177. In an interview with José Pedro Castanheira, in the edition of *Expresso Magazine* of 9 April 1994, Rui Patrício admits that he had no previous knowledge of the operation and that it was not discussed in the Council of Ministers.

99 Xavier, *Rui Patrício – A vida conta-se inteira*, p.178.

100 SHDN – GR9 Q5 122: Special Intelligence Bulletin No 11.101 of the Secrétariat Général de la Défense Nationale, Paris (27/11/1970).

101 ADN – GABMIN/007/0029/004.

102 ADN – GABMIN/007/0029/005: SECRET 548/BE 28NOV70 COMCHEFEGUINE to RPFW/DEFNAC. This request is strange given that the Air Force had no aircraft with such capabilities other than the P2V-5 Neptune, which could operate at night, but had little precision in bombing.

103 ADN – GABMIN/007/0029/005: SECRET 1117/BE 14FEV71 COMCHEFEGUINE to GENERALDEFNAC. It has not been possible to confirm the origin of these fighters, but it is known that the MiG-17 did not have the capacity for photographic reconnaissance missions. In addition, the level of operation of the Guinean Air Force was very low, and it was not very credible for Guinean pilots to risk a flight to Bissau, thus leaving doubt as to the origin of the aircraft observed.

104 ADN – GABMIN/007/0029/005.

105 The F-86 fighters had been ceded to Portugal in the context of NATO for the defence of Europe, and their relocation to Africa was not authorised because it was a region outside NATO. Even so, the fighters had been in Guinea from 1961–64 on several deployments, which led the Americans to demand their withdrawal. A new deployment was considered in 1971, but then abandoned so as not to create problems with the US. See ADN – SGDN/1REP/105/0345/003.

106 Robert H. Estabrook, 'U.N. Orders Pullout of Guinea Invaders', *The Washington Post* (23/11/1970).

107 *The New York Times*, 'Guinea Charges Further "Incursions" by Mercenaries' (25/11/1970).

108 *The New York Times*, 'Guinea Again Asks Arms to Fight Foe' (26/11/1970).

109 *The New York Times*, 'Belgian Accused in Raid Is Reported in Portugal' (26/11/1970).

110 *The Washington Post*, 'U.N. Group Hears Guinea' (27/11/1970).

111 Bertram B. Johansson, 'Portugal blast by UN called far reaching', *The Christian Science Monitor* (11/12/1970).

112 CIA Intelligence Report. *Soviet General Purpose Naval Deployments. Outside Home Waters: Characteristics and Trends* (June 1973), p.15.

113 CIA – *Impact of Soviet Naval Presence in Third World Countries, Guinea* (January 1983), pp.19–30.

114 CIA – Interagency Intelligence Memorandum – *The Significance of Soviet TU-95 Bear D Deployments in West Africa* (April 1977).

115 CIA – *Impact of Soviet Naval Presence in Third World Countries, Guinea* (January 1983), p.20.

116 Information from Alexander Rosin, who writes in Russian in his blog: http://alerozin.narod.ru/GuinBis.htm.

117 This information was sent to the Deputy Secretary of National Defence of the SGDN by the PIDE/DGS on 10 April 1973, after a request by the SGDN for research on naval means of the PAIGC. See ADN – SGDN/2REP/076/0322/003.

118 Hernandez, pp.50–51.

119 Cabral, p.361; Keita, p.287.

120 Those hanged on the bridge were Baldé Ousmane, former minister and former governor of the Central Bank; Magassouba Moriba, former minister; Barry Ibrahima, former minister; and Keita Kara, police commissioner. Cf. Gomez, p.43.

121 Diallo, *La vérité du ministre,* pp.237–257.

122 Lewin, pp.38–41.

123 SHDN – GR9 Q5 122: Special Intelligence Bulletin No 10.142 of the Secrétariat Général de la Défense Nationale, Paris (3/2/1971). André Lewin, in his biography on Sékou Touré, speaks of 62 death sentences. Cf. Lewin, p.37.

124 CIA – National Intelligence Survey, *Guinea* (May 1973), p.12.

125 CIA – National Intelligence Survey, *Guinea* (May 1973), p.12.

126 The content of this message is reproduced in Marinho, pp.167–168.

127 Rittmuller, pp.143–144.

128 Starckmann, p.135.

Chapter 4

1 AHPR – GB/GB0205/1729/056: Presentation by the Governor and Chief Commander of the Armed Forces of Guinea. Meeting of the Supreme Council of National Defence on 7 May 1971. During this meeting of the CSDN, Spínola gave a presentation on the situation in Guinea which is annexed to the report of the meeting.

2 AHPR – GB/GB0205/1729/056.

3 AHPR – GB/GB0205/1729/056.

4 AHPR – GB/GB0205/1729/056.

5 AHPR – GB/GB0205/1729/056.

6 ADN – CEMGFA/017/0037/060.

7 ADN – CEMGFA/017/0037/060.

8 ADN – CEMGFA/017/0037/060.

9 ADN – GABMIN/007/0029/005.

10 Rui Patrício, in an interview with José Pedro Castanheira, in the edition of *Expresso Magazine* of 9 April 1994, says that this meeting was arranged by the French, but that the conversation was very difficult, with recriminations on both sides. Patrício also mentions that the Senegalese minister even suggested that Portugal should grant independence to Guinea-Bissau.

11 Cunha, *O Ultramar, a Nação e o 25 de Abril*, p.48.

12 The minutes of this meeting are published in Maria José Tíscar, *A Pide no Xadrez Africano – Conversas com o Inspector Fragoso Allas,* 2nd edition (Lisbon: Edições Colibri, 2018), pp.306–313. Luso-Africans are people of mixed Portuguese and African ancestry who speak Portuguese.

13 Cunha, *Ainda o 25 de Abril*, p.96.

14 ADN – CEMGFA/017/0035/012: Note on the talks between the President of the Republic of Senegal and the Governor of Guinea on 18 May 1972.

15 Marcello Caetano, *Depoimento* (Rio de Janeiro: Distribuidora Record, 1974), p.190.

16 Marcello Caetano, *Depoimento* (Rio de Janeiro: Distribuidora Record, 1974), p.191.

17 Testimony of António de Spínola in *Os Últimos Governadores do Império* (Lisbon: Edições Neptuno, 1994), pp.73–74.

18 ADN – CEMGFA/017/0037/059: Annex A of the Report of the CEMGFA visit to Guinea, January 73.

19 ADN – CEMGFA/017/0037/059: Annex 5 of the Report of the CEMGFA visit to Guinea, January 73.

20 ADN – CEMGFA/017/0037/059: Report on CEMGFA's visit to Guinea, January 73.

21 ADN – CEMGFA/010/0023/038.

22 ADN – CEMGFA/015/0032/026: Overseas Staff Charts, 1965–1974; ADN –SGDN/1REP/092/0307/007: Exposition of the Operational Situation in the Province of Guinea (JAN 61/MAR 64), made to the High Command Course, IAEM, on 2 May 1964, Scheme No. 13.

23 José Pedro Castanheira, *Quem mandou matar Amílcar Cabral* (Lisbon: Relógio de Água Editores, 1995).

24 This episode clearly shows the lack of preparation of Guinean sailors, who could not sail at night.

25 http://alerozin.narod.ru/GuinBis.htm.

26 José Matos, 'O último ano do Fiat G.91 na Guiné', *Revista Militar* No. 4 (April 2020), pp.395–414.

27 Alexandre Coutinho e Lima, *A Retirada de Guileje – A verdade dos factos,* 3rd edition (DG Edições, 2009).

28 José de Moura Calheiros, *A última missão* (Lisbon: Caminhos Romanos, 2010).

29 ADN – CEMGFA/017/0034/004.

30 AHPR – GB/GB0205/1729/095: High Council of National Defence – Report of the session of 22 May 1973.

31 AHM – DIV/2/4/223/004: Independent Territorial Command of Guinea – Report of the 2nd Division, 1974.

32 ADN – CEMGFA/017/0034/009: CCFAG exhibition (9/3/1974).

33 António Spínola, *Portugal e o Futuro,* 5th edition (Arcádia, 1974), p.45.

34 António Spínola, *Portugal e o Futuro,* 5th edition (Arcádia, 1974), p.160.

35 António Spínola, *Portugal e o Futuro,* 5th edition (Arcádia, 1974), p.229.

36 Marcelo Caetano, *O 25 de Abril e o Ultramar – Três entrevistas e alguns testemunhos* (Lisbon: Verbo (s.d.)), pp.119–122.

About the Author

José Matos is an independent researcher of military history in Portugal with a primary interest in the operations of the Portuguese Air Force during the colonial wars in Africa, especially in Guinea. He is a regular contributor to numerous European magazines on military aviation and naval subjects, and has collaborated in the major project 'The Air Force at the end of the Empire', published in Portugal in 2018. Recently he has written two books in Portuguese, one on the former Portuguese regime's relations with South Africa and the other on the attack against Guinea-Conakry in 1970. This is his third title for Helion's Africa @War series.